Gabrielle Shiosaki

MW00856216

Photo by Jay P. Westhauser

A scene from the Milwaukee Repertory Theater production of "A Christmas Carol." Set design by Vicki Smith.

A CHRISTMAS CAROL

BY
CHARLES DICKENS

ADAPTED BY
ROMULUS LINNEY

★

★

DRAMATISTS
PLAY SERVICE
INC.

A CHRISTMAS CAROL
Copyright © 1996, Romulus Linney

All Rights Reserved

CAUTION: Professionals and amateurs are hereby warned that performance of A CHRISTMAS CAROL is subject to payment of a royalty. It is fully protected under the copyright laws of the United States of America, and of all countries covered by the International Copyright Union (including the Dominion of Canada and the rest of the British Commonwealth), and of all countries covered by the Pan-American Copyright Convention, the Universal Copyright Convention, the Berne Convention, and of all countries with which the United States has reciprocal copyright relations. All rights, including professional/amateur stage rights, motion picture, recitation, lecturing, public reading, radio broadcasting, television, video or sound recording, all other forms of mechanical or electronic reproduction, such as CD-ROM, CD-I, DVD, information storage and retrieval systems and photocopying, and the rights of translation into foreign languages, are strictly reserved. Particular emphasis is placed upon the matter of readings, permission for which must be secured from the Adapter's agent in writing.

The stage performance rights in A CHRISTMAS CAROL (other than first class rights) are controlled exclusively by DRAMATISTS PLAY SERVICE, INC., 440 Park Avenue South, New York, NY 10016. No professional or nonprofessional performance of the Play (excluding first class professional performance) may be given without obtaining in advance the written permission of DRAMATISTS PLAY SERVICE, INC., and paying the requisite fee.

Inquiries concerning all other rights should be addressed to The Gersh Agency, 130 West 42nd Street, New York, NY 10036. Attn: Peter Hagan.

SPECIAL NOTE
Anyone receiving permission to produce A CHRISTMAS CAROL is required to give credit to the Author and Adapter as sole and exclusive Author and Adapter of the Play on the title page of all programs distributed in connection with performances of the Play and in all instances in which the title of the Play appears for purposes of advertising, publicizing or otherwise exploiting the Play and/or a production thereof. The names of the Author and Adapter must appear on separate lines, in which no other names appear, immediately beneath the title and in size of type equal to 50% of the size of the largest, most prominent letter used for the title of the Play. No person, firm or entity may receive credit larger or more prominent than that accorded the Author and Adapter.

SPECIAL NOTE ON SONGS AND RECORDINGS
For performances of copyrighted songs, arrangements or recordings mentioned in this Play, the permission of the copyright owner(s) must be obtained. Other songs, arrangements or recordings may be substituted provided permission from the copyright owner(s) of such songs, arrangements or recordings is obtained; or songs, arrangements or recordings in the public domain may be substituted.

For The Milwaukee Repertory Theater
this playwright's friend for many years
with gratitude and affection

TABLE OF CONTENTS

Charles Dickens's A CHRISTMAS CAROL, adapted by Romulus Linney, was commissioned and first produced by the Milwaukee Repertory Theater (Joseph Hanreddy, Artistic Director; Dan Fallon, Managing Director), at Pabst Theater, in Milwaukee, Wisconsin, in December, 1995. It was directed by Kenneth Albers; the set design was by Vicki Smith; the costume design was by Sam Fleming; the lighting design was by Robert Jared; the composition/musical direction was by John Tanner, the choreography was by Cate Deicher; the production stage manager was Judy Berden and the assistant stage manager was Leslie Woodruff. The cast was as follows:

EBENEZER SCROOGE	James Pickering
BOB CRATCHIT	Jonathan Gillard Daly
FRED	Rex Young
GENTLEMEN	Ron Frazier, Michael LaGue
CAROLER	Erik Devine
CAROLINE	Rengin Altay
CAROLINE'S HUSBAND	Ted deChatelet
MARLEY	Stephen Hemming
THE GHOST OF CHRISTMAS PAST	Jonathan Adams
BOYS AT THE CROSSROADS	Jason Cairns, Nicolas Costantini, Erik Devine
BOY SCROOGE	Nick Sweet
FAN	Paige Colas
MR. FEZZIWIG	Michael W. Nash
YOUNG SCROOGE	Ted deChatelet
VIOLINIST	Tara McAllister-Viel
FEZZIWIG GUESTS	Ron Frazier, Michael LaGue, Marion Oberle, Mindi Penn
MRS. FEZZIWIG	Alexandra O'Karma
BELLE	Rengin Altay
FEZZIWIG DAUGHTERS	Lauren Bone, Alexis Gladd, Michelle Read
SUITORS	Jared Cyr, Aaron Neptune, Thom Penn
OLD MAN IN THE PARK	Greg Flegel

OLD WOMAN IN THE PARK .... Heather Simmons
THE GHOST OF CHRISTMAS PRESENT ..... Michael W. Nash
MRS. CRATCHIT .... Laurie Birmingham
THE CRATCHIT CHILDREN:

        PETER .... Nicolas Costantini
        BELINDA .... Sarah McQuide
        GILLIAN .... Christine Bestor
        MIRANDA .... Kathryn Bonds
        MARTHA ....Jenny Skiba
        TINY TIM .... Jonathan Garcia, Austin Young
JULIA, FRED'S WIFE .... Lauren Bone
LUCY, JULIA'S SISTER .... Rengin Altay
MR. TOPPER .... Michael LaGue
IGNORANCE .... Jason Cairns
WANT .... Heather Whyte
THE GHOST OF CHRISTMAS YET TO COME .... Jared Cyr
BUSINESSMEN .... Jonathan Adams, Ron Frazier,
                                            Michael LaGue
OLD JOE .... Stephen Hemming
CHARWOMAN .... Laurie Birmingham
UNDERTAKER'S WOMAN .... Alexandra O'Karma
LAUNDRESS .... Lauren Bone
CHRISTMAS CAROL ENSEMBLE .... Diana Boos, Jared Cyr,
                 Greg Flegel, Alexis Gladd, Tara McAllister-Viel,
Aaron Neptune, Marion Oberle, Mindi Penn, Thom Penn,
     Michelle Read, Richard Robichaux, Heather Simmons,
                                   Jonathan Wainwright

PREFACE

When the Milwaukee Repertory asked me about adapting its new A CHRISTMAS CAROL for them, I did not remember actually reading the book, nor had I seen any of its numerous stage versions. I was acquainted only with the film starring Alastair Sim, done in England years ago, which I had liked, but only dimly remembered.

So when I read A CHRISTMAS CAROL, I was able to pretend I had never heard of the great story before. I was of course amazed not only at its beauty and durability, but at its blazing theatricality. It is part HAMLET, in its devastating revelations by fantastic ghosts, part EVERYMAN, in its sure progression toward spiritual salvation, and part Charlie Chaplin, in its fun and overflowing good spirits.

There was also, I thought, something else Dickens had created, within the narrative. It is the appearance, throughout the story, of happy boys in so many guises, from the boy who wants to sing a carol to the terrible Ebenezer Scrooge at the beginning of the book, through playmates at school and youngsters elsewhere, ending with the "remarkable" boy who gets the Christmas goose for Scrooge near the end, all pointing to the famous and heart-opening Tiny Tim. It is as if a dead boy in Scrooge is being prepared for rebirth from a calcified old man. Death and Tiny Tim finally open the mind, heart and soul of Ebenezeer Scrooge, not only to Christmas, but to the joy of life.

I vowed to stick to the bones of the story as closely as I could, to take the evolution of Scrooge seriously, and to try and find, as he goes, the child within him that slowly emerges from his ordeal to such bountiful happiness.

I was excited at the prospects of a beautiful and technically dazzling production at the Pabst Theater by the Milwaukee Repertory. But I wanted to create at the same time a much simpler version, that could be played in a room, with only as much production as could be afforded or desired.

So here is the full-blown theatrical A CHRISTMAS CAROL, along with a framework and suggestions how to produce a much more modest one. Its story can fly on beautiful wings of elegant theatre, but move us just as deeply when done as simply, as cleanly and as forthrightly as the brilliant imagination of its creator, Charles Dickens.

I am indebted to Ken Albers, who directed the play brilliantly, making many crucial contributions to the script, while Joe Hanreddy gave us both helpful support, and Dan Fallon and Sara O'Connor, as always, cheered us on. I am grateful to the Milwaukee Repertory Theater, where I have experienced many happy productions of my own plays, for allowing me to adapt this version of a timeless and beloved parable. I hope that the-atres with resources great and small, like Tiny Tim, will say, "God Bless Us Every One," and each in their own way, take Scrooge over and over again on his wondrous journey.

— Romulus Linney

PRODUCTION NOTES

The sets, lights, costumes, music for the play can range from the most any theater can afford, to almost nothing.

Using the alternate framework suggested, with a small "company" that plays all the many parts and moves necessary furniture about, the play can be done anywhere, from a proscenium stage to a thrust to a black box to the floor of one end of a room.

An entrance or two are needed, which can be lit in various spooky ways for the ghosts to pass in and out of, with actors sitting around playing music, making noises, etc., during the action.

A few plain benches, chairs and wooden crates moved in various combinations by the actors can become Scrooge's bed and all other furnishings. Costumes may be the barest suggestion of the period, or not even that. The story is so strong it can not only hold up without full production, but take on a different, very effective life without it.

Using the method of doing the bare action with a few actors, A CHRISTMAS CAROL is in my opinion just as strong as a huge production with a large cast.

The LITTLE BOY LOST song that Tiny Tim sings is to the music of an old German carol, O JESULEIN SUSS by George Frederick Kaufmann, or music may be composed to fit my lyrics.

CHARACTERS

EBENEZER SCROOGE

A NAMELESS BOY

BOB CRATCHIT

TINY TIM

THE COMPANY:
MEN, WOMEN and CHILDREN OF LONDON

TIME

Awhile ago

PLACE

London, England

A CHRISTMAS CAROL

The curtain is brightly lit.

Music: warm and cheerful Christmas music, carols perhaps, but not familiar ones.

House lights go to half. Music cross fades with a rising wind. House lights go out.

Curtain rises on a dark stage. Wind.

Lights slowly discover a tombstone, with Marley written on it.

We hear a Voice: warm, avuncular, and friendly, as if talking quietly in our ear by a fire.

VOICE.   To begin with — Marley was dead. There is no doubt whatever about that. The register of his burial was signed by the clergyman, the clerk, the undertaker. Old Marley was dead as a doornail, and no doubt about it. This must be distinctly understood, or nothing wonderful can come of the story I am about to relate. *(From behind the tombstone, enter Ebenezer Scrooge walking slowly forward with his cane to the grave.)* There was only one mourner at his funeral. Ebenezer Scrooge, his partner in business. *(A sign, creaking and waving in the wind, appears and moves to hang quite mysteriously over Scrooge.)* Scrooge never painted out old Marley's name. There it hung seven long years afterward, above the warehouse door:

SCROOGE AND MARLEY. *(Scrooge stares down at the grave, impassive.)* Sometimes people called Scrooge Scrooge and sometimes they called him Marley, but he answered to both names; it was all the same to him. And seven years passed. *(Wind. Lights change. Music. The sign moves away. Scrooge takes a deep breath and moves away. The grave slides off in the other direction. Wind. Snow. Scrooge, head down in the wind, clutching his hat and his cane in the cold, begins a journey through the years to his office. The sign: SCROOGE & MARLEY goes with him, and ends up above the warehouse door.)* These seven years did not change him. Oh! He was a tightfisted hand at the grindstone, Scrooge! A squeezing, wrenching, grasping, scraping, clutching, covetous old sinner! *(Streets of London appear, backed by cut outs of London buildings, grey and dismal. People go by, rushing about in the cold, blowing on hands and stamping their feet. Tiny Tim, a crippled boy who must struggle to walk, gets in Scrooge's way. Scrooge stares at him angrily, pushes him aside with his cane, and goes on. Tim watches him, then struggles on his way. Scrooge finally arrives at his office, and enters, under the sign, SCROOGE & MARLEY, which glows with a slightly sinister light. Bob Cratchit, his clerk, works at a small desk, facing a larger one, which is Scrooge's.)*

CRATCHIT. Sir.

SCROOGE. *(Ice.)* Humph. *(Scrooge hangs up his coat, sits at his larger desk, and begins to work. Outside the office, people pass by.)* Rent! Interest! Dividend! Penalty! *(Pause, work.)* Penalty! Dividend! Interest! Rent! *(Scrooge's Nephew moves toward the office. People go by him, stamping their feet and beating their chests in the cold. Enter Nephew.)*

NEPHEW. Merry Christmas, Uncle! *(Scrooge looks up, shakes his head, looks back at his work.)* I'm delighted to see you! On such a beautiful day!

SCROOGE. It's freezing.

NEPHEW. Aren't you glad to see me? I am very fond of you.

SCROOGE. Because your mother was my sister does not mean I have to be fond of *you!*

NEPHEW. But you are! I know you are!

SCROOGE. Bah!

NEPHEW. And I say, Merry Christmas!

SCROOGE. Humbug!

NEPHEW. Christmas a humbug, Uncle? You don't mean that, I am sure.

SCROOGE. I do! *(Scrooge examines his Nephew.)* What right have you to be merry?

NEPHEW. What right have you to be dismal?

SCROOGE. What reason have you to be cheerful?

NEPHEW. What reason have you to be morose?

SCROOGE. You're poor enough!

NEPHEW. You're rich enough!

SCROOGE. Bah! Humbug!!

NEPHEW. Don't be cross, Uncle!

SCROOGE. What else can I be, when I live in such a world of fools as this! Merry Christmas! What's Christmas time to you but a time for paying bills — without money; a time for finding yourself a year older and not an hour richer. If I had my way, every idiot who goes about with "Merry Christmas" on his lips, should be boiled with his own pudding and buried with a stake of holly through his heart.

NEPHEW. Uncle!

SCROOGE. Nephew! You keep Christmas in your way and let me keep it in mine!

NEPHEW. But you don't keep it!

SCROOGE. Let me leave it alone then! Much good it does you.

NEPHEW. I have always thought of Christmas as a good time: a kind, charitable, time, when men and women open their hearts, think of others as fellow passengers to the grave, and not another race of other creatures bound on other journeys. The way, Fan, my mother and your sister, thought of it. And therefore, Uncle, though Christmas has never put a scrap of gold in my pocket, I believe that it has done me good and will do me good and I say God bless it! *(Cratchit applauds gently.)*

CRATCHIT. Bravo. *(Scrooge whirls around, glares at him.)*

SCROOGE. Another sound from YOU, and you will keep your Christmas by losing your job! *(To Nephew.)* That was a fine speech. Go into Parliament!

15

NEPHEW. Don't be angry, Uncle. Come and have Christmas dinner with us!

SCROOGE. I will see you in hell first.

NEPHEW. Why do you act like this? It is very foolish of you.

SCROOGE. Why did you get married? That was foolish of you!

NEPHEW. Because I fell in love!

SCROOGE. Because you fell in love? Good afternoon.

NEPHEW. What's wrong with falling in love?

SCROOGE. Goodbye.

NEPHEW. I want nothing from you. I ask nothing of you. Why can't we be friends!

SCROOGE. GoodBYE!

NEPHEW. I am sorry to find you so resolute. We have never had any quarrel to which I have been a party. So, a Merry Christmas, Uncle!

SCROOGE. GET — OUT!!

NEPHEW. And a Happy New Year!!!

SCROOGE. BAH, HUMBUG!!! *(The Nephew goes, and passes Cratchit.)*

NEPHEW. Merry Christmas, Mr. Cratchit!

CRATCHIT. Merry Christmas, sir! *(Nephew shakes hands with Cratchit.)*

NEPHEW. *(Going.)* Merry Christmas! *(Cratchit goes to Scrooge, holds out some papers.)*

SCROOGE. *(To Cratchit.)* And here you are, Cratchit, a clerk making fifteen shillings a week, with a wife and a hungry house full of children, saying Merry Christmas to anybody who comes in the door. *(Scrooge takes the papers.)* I'll go to an insane asylum. *(Cratchit goes back to his desk. Scrooge works. Enter Portly Gentleman 1 and Portly Gentleman 2. They carry books, papers, and a pen.)*

GENTLEMAN 1. Scrooge and Marley's, I believe?

GENTLEMAN 2. Have we the pleasure of addressing Mr. Scrooge or Mr. Marley?

SCROOGE. Mr. Marley has been dead these seven years ago today.

GENTLEMAN 2. Today?

SCROOGE.   This very night, as a matter of fact.

GENTLEMAN 1.   But the sign —

SCROOGE.   Is perfectly good as it is! Why buy another one! Gentlemen?

GENTLEMAN 1.   Our credentials, sir. *(He shows Scrooge a letter.)*

GENTLEMAN 2.   The Larger London Amalgamated Association for the Poor.

GENTLEMAN 1.   We have no doubt that Mr. Marley's liberality is well represented by his surviving partner.

SCROOGE.   Liberality?

GENTLEMAN 2.   At this festive season of the year, Mr. Scrooge, it is more than usually desirable that we should make some slight provision for the poor and destitute.

GENTLEMAN 1.   Who suffer greatly.

GENTLEMAN 2.   They need food.

GENTLEMAN 1.   They need clothing.

GENTLEMAN 2.   They need shelter.

GENTLEMAN 1.   They need the warmth of our concern.

GENTLEMAN 2.   Hundreds of thousands are in want of common comforts. *(Gentleman 1 holds out a pen. Gentleman 2 a letter pledging a contribution.)*

SCROOGE.   Are there no prisons?

GENTLEMAN 1.   Plenty of prisons.

SCROOGE.   And the workhouses?

GENTLEMAN 2.   There are many institutions in London where the poor must work like slaves.

GENTLEMAN 1.   We wish we could say there were not.

SCROOGE.   I am glad to hear it. I was afraid from what you said that something has occurred to stop them in their useful course.

GENTLEMAN 2.   Well, a few of us are endeavoring to raise a fund to buy the poor some meat and drink and means of warmth, since workhouses furnish little cheer to the multitudes.

GENTLEMAN 1.   What shall we put you down for?

SCROOGE.   Nothing.

GENTLEMAN 2.   Nothing?

GENTLEMAN 1.   You wish to be anonymous?

SCROOGE.   I wish to be left alone. I don't make myself merry at Christmas, and I can't afford to make idle people merry. I help to support the establishments I have mentioned. They cost enough and those who are badly off must go there.

GENTLEMAN 2.   Many can't go there. Many would rather die.

SCROOGE.   If they had rather die, they had better do it and decrease the surplus population. It is enough for a man to understand his own business and not to interfere with other people's. Good afternoon. *(They look at each other: a hopeless case.)*

GENTLEMAN 1.   Very well.

GENTLEMAN 2.   Good afternoon, to you, sir.

GENTLEMAN 1 and GENTLEMAN 2.   And Merry Christmas. *(Exit Gentleman 1 and Gentleman 2.)*

SCROOGE.   Humbug! *(It has been getting darker. Scrooge lights a candle. Cratchit lights a smaller one. With a flourish of renewed energy, Scrooge sets to work again, recording numbers, fiercely.)* Ah! There! Rent! There! Interest! There! Dividend! And there! Penalty! Compounded Semi-annually! There! *(Enter a ragamuffin Boy, to stand before Scrooge. He sings a carol in a quivering voice.)*

BOY.   *(Singing.)*
    NOEL, NOEL,
    NOEL, NOEL.
    BORN IS A CHILD IN ISRAEL.

SCROOGE.   What do YOU want?

BOY.   I want to sing you a carol, sir, for a penny.

SCROOGE.   And why, you miserable boy, would you presume to do that?

BOY.   It's Christmas, sir. And I'm an orphan, sir. I must sing for my supper.

SCROOGE.   An orphan?

BOY.   Yes, sir.

SCROOGE.   No mother, no father?

BOY.   No, sir.

SCROOGE.   Just a little orphan boy all alone, out in the cold, begging, wanting my money?

BOY. A little something, sir.

SCROOGE. I'll give you something, all right! *(Scrooge opens his desk drawer, seizes his ruler, comes at the Boy.)* Hold out your hand, and I'll give you this!! *(The Boy screams and runs out the door. Scrooge looks after him.)* Begging. Christmas. Orphans. Bah, humbug. *(Scrooge turns to go back to his desk, sees Bob Cratchit staring at him.)* And what are you looking at?

CRATCHIT. Nothing, Mr. Scrooge.

SCROOGE. I don't HAVE to like orphans, do I?

CRATCHIT. No, Mr. Scrooge.

SCROOGE. You can, if you want to.

CRATCHIT. Yes, Mr. Scrooge.

SCROOGE. The world can, if it wants to. BUT I DON'T HAVE TO LIKE ORPHANS!!

CRATCHIT. No, Mr. Scrooge. *(Scrooge goes to his desk. He looks at his watch.)*

SCROOGE. Seven o'clock. *(Scrooge snuffs out his candle. Cratchit snuffs out his candle. Scrooge puts on an overcoat. Cratchit puts on a comforter, since he has no overcoat.)* You'll want all day off tomorrow, I suppose?

CRATCHIT. If it's quite convenient, sir.

SCROOGE. It's NOT quite convenient, not at all, sir, and it's not fair! If I were to dock you half a crown for it, you'd think yourself ill-used!

CRATCHIT. Mr. Scrooge —

SCROOGE. But you don't think me ill-used when I pay full day's wages for no days work!

CRATCHIT. It's only once a year, sir.

SCROOGE. That's your excuse for picking my pocket every December 25th? But I suppose you must have it, the whole day. Be here all the earlier December 26th!

CRATCHIT. Yes, sir, Mr. Scrooge! Merry — *(Scrooge stares at him.)* Good afternoon, Mr. Scrooge. *(Exit Bob Cratchit, very quickly, very glad to go, whistling a carol as he vanishes. Scrooge closes his ledger book. Thunder. Lightning. In several lightning flashes, we see Scrooge coming out of his office. Wind. A young couple, Caroline and her Husband, rush to Scrooge as he leaves his office, which moves away from them as they talk.)*

CAROLINE. Mr. Scrooge!

SCROOGE. Yes?

HUSBAND. Merry Christmas, sir!

SCROOGE. What do you want?

HUSBAND. A word with you, sir!

SCROOGE. Tomorrow!

CAROLINE. Tomorrow's Christmas!

SCROOGE. I'm on my way home!

HUSBAND. We barely got here from our own work.

CAROLINE. We can't leave it, you see, and we must speak to you.

HUSBAND. It's urgent, sir!

CAROLINE. Please, sir!

SCROOGE. All right! Speak!

HUSBAND. It's about our final debt to you, sir. Our payment is due at the end of the week.

SCROOGE. Then pay it!!

CAROLINE. We can't!

SCROOGE. Then I'll see you in prison! Goodbye! (*Howling wind. Scrooge moves away from the couple. The warehouse and office has vanished, but its sign. MARLEY & SCROOGE stays in the air and follows Scrooge as he winds his way through a street, going home. Thunder, lightning, howling wind and driven snow. Scrooge's warehouse is replaced by the front of his home, a tall front door and gate before it. Scrooge goes through the gate, and walks a few steps directly D. He stops, as if he heard something. Shakes his head. Only the wind. Scrooge goes to his front door.*)

MARLEY'S VOICE. Scrooge! Scrooge!

SCROOGE. Who's there? (*No answer. Scrooge shakes his head again and takes out his key to open his front door.*)

MARLEY'S VOICE. Scrooge! Scrooge! (*Scrooge turns around again. When he does, the door of his house lights up, in a supernatural way. The knocker of his house, much larger than usual, also glows. Scrooge turns back to face his front door. Lightning. Scrooge stops, astounded. The knocker, spotlit, is alive: a face is in its place, sticking through the door. It is the face of his partner Jacob Marley. Marley's voice, amplified, reverberates around Scrooge, the words unclear.*) SCROOGE! SCROOGE! (*Lightning and thunder and dark-*

ness again. The normal light returns and the door has a plain brass knocker there without Marley's face, which has been withdrawn in the dark, replaced by a brass panel. Scrooge steps back, shakes his head.)
SCROOGE.   Bah! *(Scrooge grasps the door firmly and pushes it open.)* Nothing. Humbug. *(Scrooge closes the door and the sound reverberates all around the stage. Music. Scrooge takes a candle from his pocket, lights it and enters his house. A platform moves onstage on which is his bed, with curtains around it, a small chest for clothes and a coal grate fireplace, which glows. An old bell-pull hangs by the bed, with a little bell at the end of it. A door to one side also appears. Scrooge puts his candle on the table, and starts to takes off his clothes quickly.)* Brrr!! *(Scrooge gets off half his clothes.)* BRRRR! *(He opens his chest, takes out a nightshirt and a cap, pops them on over his trousers and shoes. He starts to take off his shoes. The bell-pull begins to sway.)* What's this? *(The bell-pull rings.)* That doesn't ring anymore! *(Scrooge grabs the bell-pull. Tugs on it once, twice. The third time it comes away and hangs loose in his hand. He shudders. He throws it into the fire. The fire flares, blazes up more fiercely.)* What's this??? *(Scrooge looks around, very uneasy. He bends over and takes off his shoes, looking up now and then to make sure he's alone. He looks under the bed, everywhere.)* Nothing to it. Humbug. *(He blows out his candle and gets into bed. He pulls the curtains around his bed shut. Pause. The bed sits there, in a dim, spooky light. Pause. A bell, from somewhere else, spectral and deep, rings. Scrooge tears open the curtains and sits up in bed.)* What's that? There's no bell like that in my house! *(The bell tolls again. Scrooge dives down under the covers. The bell tolls again, and then there is a sound of a low moan, and a clanking of chains. Scrooge pops out of the covers again.)* What's THAT? It sounds like — *(A low moaning, a rattling of chains.)* Ghosts? Humbug! I don't believe it! *(Scrooge dives down into the bed again. BOOM! The door blows open. Scrooge gets out of bed, goes carefully to the door. He looks out of it. Nothing. He steps back, closes the door. There is a terrific surge of fire in the fireplace. Out of the flames comes the Ghost of Jacob Marley. He is covered with chains which are VERY heavy and are draped all over him, along with keys, padlocks, and heavy metal purses. Scrooge turns and sees him.)* Ah! *(Marley's mouth stays wide open, the jaw fallen in death. Around his neck is a black kerchief.)*

Who are you? *(Marley's Ghost just stares at him.)* Do I know you? *(Marley's Ghost slowly nods.)* Are you a ghost? *(Marley's Ghost nods.)* Can you speak? *(Marley's Ghost nods again, and slowly ties the black kerchief around his neck and under his chin, holding up his jaw.)* What do you want with me?

MARLEY. Much!

SCROOGE. Who are you?

MARLEY. Ask me who I was.

SCROOGE. Who were you then?

MARLEY. In life, I was your partner, Jacob Marley.

SCROOGE. Jacob? *(Peering.)* Well, you look *something* like him.

MARLEY. You don't believe in me?

SCROOGE. I do not.

MARLEY. Why do you doubt your senses?

SCROOGE. Because a little thing affects them. A slight disorder of the stomach deranges them. You may be a bit of undigested beef, a blot of mustard, a crumb of cheese, a fragment of an underdone potato. There's more gravy than grave about you, whatever you are!

MARLEY. *(Screaming.)* AHHHHHH! *(A frightful sound! MARLEY jumps up and down, crying out in pain, shaking his chains, while the sound of his chains and his crying and groaning are magnified into a shattering noise.)*

SCROOGE. Mercy, mercy, dreadful apparition!

MARLEY. DO you believe in me NOW?

SCROOGE. I do! I must! But why do you walk the earth, and why do you come to me?

MARLEY. It is required of every man that the spirit within him should walk among his fellow men. It is doomed to wander through the world — oh, woe is me! — to see the misery it has caused and the happiness it cannot share.

SCROOGE. You are fettered. Tell me why?

MARLEY. I wear the chain I forged in life. I made it link by link, and yard by yard. I put it on of my own free will, and of my own free will, I wore it. Is it strange to you? Your chain was as full and heavy and as long as this one seven Christmas eves ago. You have labored on it since, and it is even longer now.

SCROOGE.   Old Jacob Marley. Speak comfort to me, Jacob.

MARLEY.   I have none to give. My spirit never walked beyond our counting house — MARK ME! — and now, weary journeys lie before me. No rest, no peace. Only the incessant torture of remorse.

SCROOGE. But why? You were always a good man of business, Jacob.

MARLEY.   *(Screaming.)* BUSINESS?? *(Marley rattles his chains and makes his dreadful noise again, even louder. Scrooge, on his knees, shrinks back.)* MANKIND was my business!! The common welfare was my business! Charity! Mercy! Mercy! Forbearance, and benevolence, were all my business! *(Marley holds up his chains at arm's length, and as if they were the cause of his grief, dashes them to the floor beside Scrooge, making him shudder.)* At this time of the year, I suffer most! *(Marley reaches out and grabs Scrooge's shoulders.)* Hear me! My time is nearly gone!

SCROOGE.   I will! But don't be too hard upon me! And Jacob, don't be FLOWERY, Jacob, please!

MARLEY.   *(Rattles chains.)* I WILL BE FLOWERY!! I am here tonight to give you a solemn warning, you have only one chance of escaping my fate.

SCROOGE.   Yes! Yes! You were always a good friend to me, Jacob!

MARLEY.   You will be haunted by Three Spirits.

SCROOGE.   Is that the chance you mentioned?

MARLEY.   Take it!

SCROOGE.   I think I'd rather not.

MARLEY.   Without their visits, you cannot hope to shun the path I tread. Expect the first tonight, when the bell tolls one. SCROOGE. Couldn't I take them all at once and get it over with, Jacob? *(Marley takes up his kerchief-wrapper again, and begins to tie his jaw back up tighter.)*

MARLEY.   Expect the second when the bell tolls two. The third when the bell tolls three. *(He moves back toward the door.)* And for your own sake, remember what has passed between us! Look to see me no more! *(Fire surges in the fireplace, into which Marley vanishes. Scrooge jumps into bed again. He pulls the curtains shut all around the bed. Pause. Long pause. A bell tolls one. Pause. Scrooge looks out of his curtains.)*

SCROOGE.   Nobody. Good! *(He shuts his curtains again. Dim light. Bed curtains at the foot of the bed fly open. Scrooge sits up, terrified. Curtains on the right, then the left fly open. Scrooge doesn't know what to do. There is a change of light, into a dazzling brilliance. It is quick, like a pistol shot. A hand reaches between the curtains behind Scrooge's head and whips them open. Scrooge crawls down to the floor of his bed and stares at the apparition at its head. Revealed is a strange figure, the Ghost of Christmas Past. He is a man in white, ascetic and stern, with skin pink and healthy but with long, snow white hair that hangs down his back. He seems ageless. He holds a branch of green holly in his hands, but he is draped all over with beautiful summer flowers. Most astonishing of all is the incredible brilliance of the light that surrounds the Ghost of Christmas Past now when he appears and will later, when from time to time, he will point things out to Scrooge. It might be an almost audience-blinding light, like a klieg light, or a lighthouse Fresnel searchlight. Now, it is blinding Scrooge.)* Ah! I can't see! *(The light returns to normal.)*

CHRISTMAS PAST.   Is that better?

SCROOGE.   Yes. You blinded me.

CHRISTMAS PAST.   The light I bring you is bright, for it must see into very dark places.

SCROOGE.   Are you the spirit, sir, whose coming was foretold to me?

CHRISTMAS PAST.   I am!

SCROOGE.   Who and what are you?

CHRISTMAS PAST.   I am the Ghost of Christmas Past.

SCROOGE.   Long past?

CHRISTMAS PAST.   No, your past.

SCROOGE.   Why are you here?

CHRISTMAS PAST.   Your welfare.

SCROOGE.   Thank you very much, but the best thing for me would be a good night's sleep.

CHRISTMAS PAST.   Your reclamation then!

SCROOGE.   Reclamation? From what?

CHRISTMAS PAST.   From yourself! Rise and walk with me. *(The light again, blinding Scrooge again, who jumps out of bed, stands shivering in his night gown and cap.)*

SCROOGE. I can't see!

CHRISTMAS PAST. You will! Take my hand.

SCROOGE. Where are we going?

CHRISTMAS PAST. Give me your hand. *(Scrooge gives the Ghost of Christmas Past his hand. Darkness. Music. Scrooge's house moves off. Whirling lights. Scrooge and the Ghost of Christmas Past seem to fly through the air as the lights whirl around them. For a second, the brilliant light. Then normal light. The bedroom has disappeared. Scrooge and the Ghost of Christmas Past stand by crossroads signs, larger than life, pointing four ways. A Boy, Scrooge as a Boy, with a book, stands behind the window of a schoolroom looking at the signs. In the background appear trees and clouds. Music ends.)*

SCROOGE. Good heavens! The crossroads!

CHRISTMAS PAST. You remember it?

SCROOGE. Of course! That way was — school — and that way was — the town and — why, that way was home! I was born here! I was a boy in this place! *(Enter Orson and Valentine. They are racing to the crossroads, from school. Scrooge as a Boy leaves his window and runs after them.)*

ORSON. I'll get there first!

VALENTINE. No, you won't, Orson!

ORSON. I will, Valentine!

SCROOGE AS A BOY. No, I will!!

ORSON and VALENTINE. Ebenezer!

SCROOGE. There I am! *(Orson almost gets to the sign, reaches out to touch it. Valentine grabs him and pulls him back, tries to touch it himself. Scrooge as a Boy grabs <u>him</u> and pulls him back. Their game is to keep each other from touching the sign post, until all, piling on top of each other, grab the sign post. Scrooge as a Boy first.)*

ORSON. I got it!

VALENTINE. *(Simultaneous.)* I got it!

SCROOGE AS A BOY. *(Simultaneous.)* I got it! *(They all collapse on top of each other in affectionate roughhouse, in front of Scrooge and the Ghost of Christmas Past.)*

VALENTINE. I win!

ORSON. No, I win!!

SCROOGE AS A BOY. We all win!!!

ALL.   WHEEEE!!

SCROOGE.   Boys. Roughhouse.

CHRISTMAS.   You were one of them.

ORSON.   Well, fellows, here come my mother and father. Merry Christmas to you.

VALENTINE.   Merry Christmas! *(Enter the fathers and mothers of Orson and Valentine. They hold out their arms and their sons run to them.)*

ORSON.   See you next year!

VALENTINE.   See you then! *(They go off with their parents.)*

SCROOGE AS A BOY.   *(Quietly.)* Goodbye.

SCROOGE.   *(Quietly.)* Goodbye. *(Scrooge as a Boy goes back to the window of the schoolroom with a small desk. He sits at the desk, and with a little notebook, adds up simple numbers.)*

SCROOGE AS A BOY.   One hundred seventy-eight, one hundred seventy-nine, one hundred eighty. *(Scrooge looks at him through the window.)*

SCROOGE.   I had forgotten this. *(Scrooge as a Boy pauses. He sighs, rubs his eyes, then goes back to his work.)* One hundred eighty-one, one hundred eighty-two — *(He counts on.)*

CHRISTMAS PAST.   Why are you still in school when all the other boys have gone home?

SCROOGE.   I lived at the school then.

CHRISTMAS PAST.   Why?

SCROOGE.   My father. He didn't want me at home. *(To Scrooge as a Boy.)* But come now, BOY! DON'T CRY!!! *(But Scrooge as a Boy does cry. Then, to comfort himself, he sings to himself.)*

SCROOGE AS A BOY.   *(Singing.)*

> NOEL, NOEL,
>
> NOEL, NOEL.
>
> BORN IS A CHILD IN ISRAEL.

CHRISTMAS PAST.   What is it?

SCROOGE.   Nothing. Nothing.

SCROOGE AS A BOY.   *(Singing.)*

> NOEL, NOEL
>
> NOEL, NOEL.

SCROOGE.   There was an orphan boy singing a carol at my

door last night. *(Scrooge as a Boy wipes his tears away and goes to work again.)*

SCROOGE AS A BOY.   One hundred ninety-four, one hundred ninety-five —

VOICE OF SCROOGE.   And what do YOU want?

VOICE OF A BOY.   Sing you a carol, sir.

VOICE OF SCROOGE.   I don't like orphans!!

SCROOGE AS A BOY.   One hundred ninety-nine, two hundred. Two hundred and one — *(Enter Fan, Scrooge's older sister. She is a woman of at least twenty years of age, rather plain but warm and understanding.)*

FAN.   Hello, Ebenezer.

SCROOGE AS A BOY.   Fan! What are you doing here?

FAN.   I've come to see you.

SCROOGE AS A BOY.   Well, here I am. At my desk at school while everybody else goes home.

FAN.   I know.

SCROOGE AS A BOY.   Father says my work is unsatisfactory. I neglect my numbers. I neglect facts and hard reality.

FAN.   I know.

SCROOGE AS A BOY.   I want to play games all the time, like a silly schoolboy, instead of learning to work, like my father's son! Oh Fan!

FAN.   Hush, Ebenezer, and listen to me. Our father is harsh, but it is because he wants us to be strong. He is mistaken, but only that.

SCROOGE AS A BOY.   He just doesn't like me.

FAN.   In his own way, he does. You know I do.

SCROOGE AS A BOY.   I do know that! You are the kindest and best older sister a boy ever had! I am so glad to see you! But I still don't know why you came.

FAN.   To bring you home.

SCROOGE AS A BOY.   Home, but father —

FAN.   I told him he couldn't treat you this way, and he agreed. So come home, with me. We'll be all together at Christmas and have the merriest time in the world!

SCROOGE AS A BOY.   You did this for me? Home?

FAN. Finish your numbers and we'll go.
SCROOGE AS A BOY. I'll never forget you, doing this for me.
SCROOGE. And I never have. Never.
FAN. Hurry.
SCROOGE AS A BOY. All right! *(Fan sits with him as he finishes writing up a last set of numbers.)*
SCROOGE. Dearest Fan.
CHRISTMAS PAST. A fine young woman.
SCROOGE. My wonderful older sister. She was warm but delicate. Never strong.
CHRISTMAS PAST. Her heart was!
SCROOGE. Yes. Her heart was very strong.
CHRISTMAS PAST. She died, I believe.
SCROOGE. And a part of me died with her.
CHRISTMAS PAST. She had children?
SCROOGE. Only one.
CHRISTMAS PAST. Your nephew?
SCROOGE. My nephew, Fred.
VOICE OF NEPHEW. Uncle!
VOICE OF SCROOGE. Nephew!
VOICE OF NEPHEW. Why do you act like this?
VOICE OF SCROOGE. Why did you get married?
VOICE OF NEPHEW. I fell in love!
VOICE OF SCROOGE. Love? Humbug!
SCROOGE AS A BOY. There! I'm finished!
FAN. Then let's go home, Ebenezer!
SCROOGE AS A BOY. Yes, Fan! Home! *(They run off.)*
SCROOGE. Fan! Fan! How good she was! How loving she was! Oh, Fan!
CHRISTMAS PAST. Come, give me your hand. *(Scrooge does. Darkness, whirling light. Wind. Scrooge and the Ghost of Christmas Past, lights whirling around them, are flying through the air. Against the sky appear cutouts and images of London again.)*
SCROOGE. I see London again!
CHRISTMAS PAST. Indeed you do. Guess what you see in London?
SCROOGE. Just London! Huge, strange, nothing like it

London!

CHRISTMAS PAST.   Look closer! Down there! What do you see?

SCROOGE.   Well, I see factories and warehouses and oh! *(A sign appears: FEZZIWIG ENTERPRISES. Below it a counting house the same as Scrooge's at the beginning of the play, but larger and warmer and more cheerful, moves onto the stage. Scrooge and the Ghost of Christmas Past go to meet it.)*

CHRISTMAS PAST.   Do you know this place?

SCROOGE.   Know it? I was apprenticed there. I learned business here!

CHRISTMAS PAST.   From who?

SCROOGE.   Why, from old Fezziwig, that's who. *(At a very tall desk is Fezziwig, working like Scrooge at the beginning of the play. But he is fat and pink and very jolly, wearing a comical cap made of colored wool.)* Old Fezziwig, bless his heart! Alive again! Old Fezziwig! I learned everything from him!

CHRISTMAS PAST.   Everything, Mr. Scrooge?

SCROOGE.   Yes! And more! I even became — in time — well, never mind.

CHRISTMAS PAST.   A better businessman?

SCROOGE.   Yes.

CHRISTMAS PAST.   Than Fezziwig?

SCROOGE.   Yes!

CHRISTMAS PAST.   That is to say, you made more money?

SCROOGE.   Much more! And what's wrong with that? Making money is not against the law, is it? *(A young man, Scrooge as a Young Man, brings Fezziwig some papers to sign, and stands waiting. Fezziwig takes out his pocket watch.)*

FEZZIWIG.   Seven o'clock.

SCROOGE AS A YOUNG MAN.   Yes, sir.

FEZZIWIG.   I suppose you'll want the whole day tomorrow.

SCROOGE AS A YOUNG MAN.   Yes, sir.

FEZZIWIG.   Do you think that's fair?

SCROOGE AS A YOUNG MAN.   It's only once a year, sir.

FEZZIWIG.   Well, sir, I will tell you this. You will not go home tonight! You will stay right here in this office! Do you hear that, sir?

SCROOGE AS A YOUNG MAN. Yes, sir.

FEZZIWIG. You will stay right here and work! And I have someone who is going to work with you! When you see this person, you will understand, sir, how hard I mean for you to work, Christmas or no Christmas! Belle, come in! *(Enter Belle, a beautiful young woman.)*

SCROOGE. Belle.

FEZZIWIG. Belle, this is young Mr. Scrooge.

BELLE. How do you do, Mr. Scrooge?

SCROOGE AS A YOUNG MAN. Very well, thank you.

FEZZIWIG. Do you understand now, Mr. Scrooge?

SCROOGE AS A YOUNG MAN. No, sir.

FEZZIWIG. Mrs. Fezziwig! Children! It's Christmas Eve, Ebenezer! *(Fezziwig hops down from his desk.)* Yo ho, yo ho! No more work tonight! Up with the shutters! On with lights! In with the family! In with the neighbors! Let's have wine! Let's have music! Let's have a dance! Hurray! It's Christmas! *(Enter Mrs. Fezziwig, as plump and pink as her husband and as colorfully dressed, all one great substantial smile.)*

MRS. FEZZIWIG. Mr. Fezziwig!!

FEZZIWIG. My dear! You know my clerk, young Mr. Scrooge.

MRS. FEZZIWIG. Indeed I do. How has my husband been treating you, Mr. Scrooge?

SCROOGE. Very well.

SCROOGE AS A YOUNG MAN. Very well, Mrs. Fezziwig.

MRS. FEZZIWIG. Have you met our cousin, Belle?

SCROOGE. Yes, I have.

SCROOGE AS A YOUNG MAN. Yes, I have.

BELLE. Mr. Fezziwig was playing a joke on Mr. Scrooge.

SCROOGE AS A YOUNG MAN. I enjoyed it very much.

FEZZIWIG. Ah! You see! There's life in the young man, after all! Very gallant, Scrooge. Belle?

BELLE. Very gallant.

MRS. FEZZIWIG. So don't let my husband work you to death, Mr. Scrooge!

SCROOGE AS A YOUNG MAN. No, ma'am.

MRS. FEZZIWIG. There's more to life than that! *(A burst of giggles and a great flouncing of lace and an entrance of young people.)* There are your daughters, sir! *(Enter three Fezziwig daughters, as colorful, ungainly, smiling and lovable as their mother and father, with three young suitors, and as many other clerks, friends, as possible, including a Man with a Violin.)*

FEZZIWIG DAUGHTERS. Merry Christmas, Papa!

FEZZIWIG. Merry Christmas, my darlings!

MRS. FEZZIWIG. Now, sir?

FEZZIWIG. Now, madame?

MRS. FEZZIWIG. Are you going to ask me for this dance, or do I box your ears?

FEZZIWIG DAUGHTERS. Box his ears!

FEZZIWIG. *(Quickly.)* Madame, may I have the honor of this dance?

MRS. FEZZIWIG. You may, sir! *(The Man with a Violin begins to play. Music. All but Scrooge as a Young Man dance: hands half round and back again the other way, down the middle and up again, in whatever joyful, clumsy, bumping, affectionate manner seems right. Scrooge, watching, begins to tap his foot. Scrooge as a Young Man, begins to tap his foot. Mrs. Fezziwig stops the dance.)* Your clerk!

FEZZIWIG. Scrooge?

MRS. FEZZIWIG. He's not dancing!

FEZZIWIG. Then he shall!

SCROOGE AS A YOUNG MAN. No, sir!

FEZZIWIG. Why not?

SCROOGE AS A YOUNG MAN. I can't!

MRS. FEZZIWIG. You must!

ALL BUT SCROOGE AS A YOUNG MAN. It's Christmas!

SCROOGE AS A YOUNG MAN. But I can't!

FEZZIWIG. You must!

SCROOGE. Yes! You must!

SCROOGE AS A YOUNG MAN. I don't know how!

BELLE. Would you like to dance with me?

SCROOGE. Yes!

BELLE. I will teach you, if I can.

SCROOGE. Go! Do it!!

SCROOGE AS A YOUNG MAN. Thank you.

BELLE. Belle.

SCROOGE AS A YOUNG MAN. Belle. *(Scrooge as a Young*

Man dances with Belle as they all go at it again. Very suddenly, the music stops. The dancers freeze in place. Scrooge rushes to them, pointing them out to the Ghost of Christmas Past.)

SCROOGE.   Look at them! Look at them! I know them all! There's Valentine, and his wild brother Orson — he was at the crossroads, he's all grown up now — and the three Fezziwig daughters, silly but good at heart, and generous, all these people, and there are the lads they will marry, so pleasant and friendly, and Mr. Fezziwig and Mrs. Fezziwig, all dancing! With me!

CHRISTMAS PAST.   How many times have you danced since?

SCROOGE.   Never! But I will again! NOW! *(The dancers come to life, and have a final go round of the dance, with great zest, getting stronger and stronger. This dance catches them up and they and we exult in it. Then, dancers exhausted, the dance ends. Mr. and Mrs. Fezziwig go to the door and shake hands with everyone as they leave. Scrooge is last. Mrs. Fezziwig kisses him on the cheek. Fezziwig shakes his hand, and goes. Belle and Scrooge as a Young Man are left alone.)*

BELLE.   I must go, too.

SCROOGE AS A YOUNG MAN.   I know. I was very glad to meet you.

BELLE.   Is that all?

SCROOGE AS A YOUNG MAN.   I beg your pardon?

BELLE.   Would you like to meet me again?

SCROOGE.   YES!!

SCROOGE AS A YOUNG MAN.   I would.

BELLE.   You are very serious. But when you danced with me, you were quite lively. Did you enjoy it?

SCROOGE.   Oh, God, yes!!!

SCROOGE AS A YOUNG MAN.   I did.

BELLE.   Then can we dance again?

SCROOGE.   Madly! Wildly! Forever and ever!!

SCROOGE AS A YOUNG MAN.   I would like that.

BELLE.   And go for walks? And talk? Do you like the parks?

SCROOGE.   I worship the parks!

SCROOGE AS A YOUNG MAN.   Yes, I do.

BELLE.   Picnics?

SCROOGE. Ah! Picnics! Ah!!

SCROOGE AS A YOUNG MAN. Yes, I do.

BELLE. Good! Then we will do all that! And I will get to know you, Mr. Scrooge, and why you are so serious, and why, in spite of that, I like you so much! *(Belle kisses Scrooge as a Young Man on the cheek and exits.)*

SCROOGE. Bliss! Bliss!!!

CHRISTMAS PAST. You? In bliss?

SCROOGE. Yes! For once in my life! Yes! *(Exit Scrooge as a Young Man, smiling, with a little skip. Scrooge and the Ghost of Christmas Past alone are onstage, in the empty office.)* Ah!

CHRISTMAS PAST. What's the matter?

SCROOGE. My clerk, Bob Cratchit.

CHRISTMAS PAST. What about him?

SCROOGE. I would like to say a word or two to him, that's all. *(Fezziwig's office moves away.)*

CHRISTMAS PAST. Why did you think of that just now?

SCROOGE. I saw myself happy just now. Cratchit is poor, you know, but he is happy. I can tell. I think that's why I am sometimes hard on him.

CHRISTMAS PAST. It is not impossible that you are learning something. But my time grows short. Quick. *(The office is replaced by a park, with a circular fountain, which has at its center, on a pedestal, the marble statue of a boy playing with a ball. Snow falls.)* Look there. *(Strolling on slowly are Scrooge Older with a Belle, older now, in a plain dark dress. Scrooge Older is in his thirties, not yet harsh and rigid, in the prime of his life, but already showing signs of greed, restlessness and cynicism that will come. They approach to the circular fountain, and walk around it, talking to each other, saying things we cannot hear.)* She too is poor. But you aren't, not anymore.

SCROOGE. Belle! She was so lovely!

CHRISTMAS PAST. And so good to you?

SCROOGE. Yes, she was!

CHRISTMAS PAST. Were you happy together?

SCROOGE. For such a long time!

CHRISTMAS PAST. On walks in the park.

SCROOGE. Planning to marry! *(Scrooge Older and Belle keep strolling around the fountain.*) Ah! That's what we did! Together!

BELLE. Marry? I wanted that more than anything. I fell quite in love with you, my dear, right at that dance. I loved your awkwardness, your shyness, and I thought, your preference for me.

SCROOGE OLDER. You were right. I did prefer you.

BELLE. You did then.

SCROOGE OLDER. And do now!

BELLE. But it makes no difference now.

SCROOGE OLDER. No difference? That I love you before all others?

BELLE. Before all other women, yes, I believe that.

SCROOGE OLDER. Then marry me!

BELLE. Women in love know they have other rivals.

SCROOGE OLDER. I can't imagine who.

BELLE. Ebenezer, you can't imagine at all. You can't see it.

SCROOGE OLDER. Don't be vague. See what?

BELLE. You have left me.

SCROOGE OLDER. I have not! My love for you is stronger than ever!

BELLE. Your love for me is one thing. But there is another love. It seemed natural at first. But it became passionate, fierce, and consuming, and it is for someone else.

SCROOGE OLDER. That is not true!

SCROOGE. And it wasn't! I loved her! With all my heart! *(A Boy comes running around the fountain.)*

BOY. Sing you a carol? *(Sings.)*
	NOEL, NOEL.

SCROOGE OLDER. Good afternoon!

BELLE. No, let's listen.

BOY. *(Singing.)*
	NOEL, NOEL —

SCROOGE OLDER. Not now!! Good afternoon, boy!

BOY. *(Singing.)*
	NOEL, NOEL —

SCROOGE OLDER. Stop it!! We don't want to hear your song! Goodbye!

BOY. All right, all right.

SCROOGE.   I wasn't foolish! I wasn't sentimental! I did love her! I did want her! *(The Boy runs off around the fountain.)*
BELLE.   You didn't have to shout at the boy.
SCROOGE OLDER.   Boys like that upset me. I don't know why. I'm sorry. But all this nonsense about my having other loves is not true!
BELLE.   Not true? Of course it's true. Your face was so smooth and unlined when I met you just a few years ago. Now it's hard and it's twisted.
SCROOGE OLDER.   Twisted? My face?
BELLE.   With desire, with passion, and with love, Ebenezer.
SCROOGE OLDER.   Yes, love for you! This is humbug! There's no other woman!
BELLE.   Oh, there is. She is called Idol. She has slowly displaced me. So be it. If she can cheer you and comfort you in time to come, as I would have tried to do, I will be glad for you.
SCROOGE OLDER.   Oh, please! What Idol has displaced you?
BELLE.   A golden one.
SCROOGE OLDER.   You mean money?
BELLE.   Yes. I mean Money.
SCROOGE OLDER.   Now you're being silly.
BELLE.   I have never been more serious in my life.
SCROOGE OLDER.   Belle, we must have courage and live life as it is! There is nothing as treacherous as poverty.
BELLE.   Courage is not what I see in you.
SCROOGE OLDER.   What do you see in me?
SCROOGE.   The future is a terrible thing, Spirit! I only wanted to protect us both!
CHRISTMAS PAST.   Listen!
BELLE.   What I see in you is fear.
SCROOGE OLDER.   Of what?
BELLE.   Of the world. Of age. Of being an old man. Yes, life can be harsh and cruel. But you are too anxious to put yourself beyond being poor, by making yourself so rich. I have watched your noble aspirations fall away, while the real love of your life, Getting Things, devours you.
SCROOGE OLDER.   If I have grown wise enough to put

things aside for later life, what's wrong with that? I still love you.

BELLE.   No, Ebenezer, you don't.

SCROOGE.   I do! I do!

BELLE.   We first loved when we were poor, content to be poor until by normal industry we could better ourselves. You've gone much faster than that. And you have changed.

SCROOGE OLDER.   Since I was a boy, yes!

BELLE.   No, since then.

SCROOGE OLDER.   I am no longer young, that's true!

BELLE.   But I still am. I know what I must do.

SCROOGE.   Don't! Belle!

BELLE.   I will release you from your vows.

SCROOGE.   You see, Spirit? From that! I wanted to protect her, from that!

SCROOGE OLDER.   Is that what you will do? Walk in this park, alone and poor?

BELLE.   And if I did, would you court me then?

SCROOGE OLDER.   You are very sure I would not.

BELLE.   I wish I wasn't. Even if you did marry a poor woman for love, I know that regret would soon follow. I let you go. With my heart full of love for the man you once were.

SCROOGE.   And still am! Still am! *(Scrooge Older starts to say something, then turns his back on her.)*

BELLE.   It may hurt for a while. But a very short while. You will be glad you did not marry a woman who would hold you back, just because you loved her.

SCROOGE.   And still do! Still do! *(Belle smiles but speaks very firmly.)*

BELLE.   We are at a crossroads, Ebenezer. One road leads one way, one another.

SCROOGE.   Belle.

BELLE.   Only you can decide where you will go. Only I can decide where I will go.

SCROOGE.   Belle, please!

BELLE.   I hope with all my heart that your way will be as right for you as I know mine is for me.

SCROOGE.   Wait! Don't!

BELLE.   Goodbye, my dear, and may God bless you. *(Belle touches Scrooge Older on the shoulder and walks away from him.)*
SCROOGE.   Turn around! You fool, she's leaving you! Turn around! *(Belle is gone. Scrooge Older turns around.)*
SCROOGE OLDER.   So be it!! *(He strides off, in the opposite direction.)*
SCROOGE.   Belle! Come back! COME BACK!!!! Ah, Spirit! Stop torturing me! Take me home!
CHRISTMAS PAST.   One shadow more!
SCROOGE.   No more! I can't stand it! *(Snow begins to fall heavily. The Ghost of Christmas Past backs away from Scrooge, leaving him at the circular railing of the fountain, beneath the statue of the little boy playing with a ball.)*
CHRISTMAS PAST.   ONE MORE! *(We hear a tiny voice singing. Enter the Boy again, singing the carol again. From the other side of the stage, enter Scrooge as a Boy. They sing together. Light on the statue of the little boy playing with a ball.)*
SCROOGE.   That boy!
BOY and SCROOGE AS A BOY.   *(Singing.)*
    NOEL, NOEL,
    NOEL, NOEL.
    BORN IS A CHILD IN ISRAEL.
SCROOGE.   And *that* boy! Who is he? What are they doing here? Why are they tormenting me?
BOY and SCROOGE AS A BOY.   *(Singing.)*
    NOEL, NOEL —
SCROOGE.   Stop it!! STOP IT!!!! *(Scrooge leans against the fountain, in furious denial. He cries out with all his powers.)* HUMBUG!!!! HUMBUG!!! HUMBUG!!!! *(The statue of boy looms above him. Boys sing. Snow falls. Curtain, very slowly.)*

END OF ACT ONE

ACT TWO

*Music that blends into "Noel, Noel" which blends into the
voice of the Boy singing.*

*Scrooge's bedroom. Dim light. The bed is curtained round.
A meager fire in the grate.*

*Scrooge is standing exactly where the fountain was, but he
is in the middle of his bedroom.*

SCROOGE.   HUMBUG!! HUM — *(Pause. Scrooge blinks his
eyes.)* Oh. What am I doing? *(He looks around, amazed.)* Walking. In my sleep! *(Pause.)* I'm cold! Bed!! *(Scrooge jumps into
bed and closes the curtains. Pause. The bell tolls the quarter hour.
We hear Marley's Voice amplified.)*
MARLEY.   *(V.O.)* SCROOOOGE!
SCROOGE.   *(Behind bed curtains.)* Oh, no! *(The bell tolls the
half hour.)*
MARLEY.   *(V.O.)* SCROOOOOOOGE! *(Scrooge sticks his head
out of the curtains.)*
SCROOGE.   Marley? Jacob? *(The bell tolls the three quarter hour.
Pause.)* Nobody there. No Jacob. No ghost. Humbug! Such a
lot of nonsense!! *(He pulls his head in again. The bell tolls twice.
Pause. The fire in the grate blazes up. A strange humming sound.
Holly, mistletoe and ivy descend, draping the walls of the bedroom.
From ropes or strings hang also long wreaths of sausages, mince pies,
strings of chestnuts, red apples and juicy oranges, cakes and pies and
plum puddings: all the largess of Christmas, with little mirrors hanging with them, making everything sparkle. Scrooge slowly looks out,
sees it all, and very slowly emerges from behind the bed curtains. He
stands in the middle of his bedroom, staring at all the marvelous
Christmas things suspended in the air around him. The strange humming noise reaches a crescendo. The bed curtains whip back, reveal-*

ing the Ghost of Christmas Present climbing out of the head of the bed. He hops down onto the floor. He is a gigantic healthy pink pagan figure, dressed in a huge, loose deep green robe, trimmed with white fur. The humming sound stops.) AHHH!

CHRISTMAS PRESENT.   Merry Christmas!

SCROOGE.   Oh, God, another one?

CHRISTMAS PRESENT.   I am the Ghost of Christmas Present.

SCROOGE.   What am I supposed to say? How do you do?

CHRISTMAS PRESENT.   Have you never seen the likes of me before?

SCROOGE.   Never!

CHRISTMAS PRESENT.   Aren't you glad to see me?

SCROOGE.   No!

CHRISTMAS PRESENT.   Why not? I'm quite a jolly fellow.

SCROOGE.   Your comrade of the Past didn't make me feel jolly. I don't think you will, either.

CHRISTMAS PRESENT.   Has any man, ever, made you feel jolly? Or woman? Or child?

SCROOGE.   No.

CHRISTMAS PRESENT.   Then try a ghost. Are you ready to go where I will take you?

SCROOGE.   Yes — and no, Spirit!

CHRISTMAS PRESENT.   Yes and no?

SCROOGE.   I protest! I have been haunted against my will.

CHRISTMAS PRESENT.   Do you regret it? Be honest!

SCROOGE.   Well, not entirely. I did learn something.

CHRISTMAS PRESENT.   But was it enough? Back in your bed, you became your old self again, doubting everything, sneering at everything.

SCROOGE.   Well, that's how I've lived! It's hard to change! All these years, I've been, well — bah, humbug!!

CHRISTMAS PRESENT.   Are you afraid now that some things may *not* be humbug?

SCROOGE.   Sometimes!

CHRISTMAS PRESENT.   That should frighten you more than anything. But you must understand what you have been!

SCROOGE.   That's hard!

CHRISTMAS PRESENT.   And you must see what you must become!

SCROOGE.   That's even harder!

CHRISTMAS PRESENT.   Try!! Here, touch my robe.

SCROOGE.   What will you do to me?

CHRISTMAS PRESENT.   I will help you to see all the things you must see, Ebenezer Scrooge, if you wish to say you have lived at all.

SCROOGE.   Lived? Of course I've lived!

CHRISTMAS PRESENT.   And *want* to live!

SCROOGE.   Of course I *want* to live!!

CHRISTMAS PRESENT.   Then touch my robe! *(Scrooge takes hold of the flowing robe. Music. A wild display of on and off lights, which become finally a sky full of very bright stars. The Christmas largess suspended in the air is replaced by the humble wash of a poor home: faded clothes and sheets. The hearth of a small, very poor house appears, in the house of Bob Cratchit, Scrooge's clerk. A few rickety chairs, an old table, peeling plaster, long faded in color. Over the small fire, several pots are boiling. Everything is very cramped and very crooked and very poor and very shabby and very jolly. Scrooge and the Ghost of Christmas Present stand beside it. Discovered at the hearth is Mrs. Bob Cratchit. She is poorly dressed but bravely be-ribboned, as is her daughter, Belinda Cratchit, about thirteen, who is laying out plain chipped pewter mugs and plates on the table. Peter Cratchit, about twelve, is wrestling with his also threadbare but proud clothes.)*

MRS. CRATCHIT.   Hurry up, Peter. Help your sister.

PETER.   Ah, this collar!

MRS. CRATCHIT.   Breathe in and hold it, then fasten it.

PETER.   Ah — hup! *(He breathes in and holds it and tries to fasten his collar. In run two smaller Cratchit daughters, Gillian and Miranda, screaming.)*

GILLIAN and MIRANDA.   The goose! The goose! We smell the goose!

PETER.   Ouf! My breath!

GILLIAN.   Your collar!

MIRANDA.   Why don't you fasten it?

PETER.   I'm trying!!

GILLIAN.   Mother, mother, we were all the way outside and we smelled the goose and knew it was ours!

MIRANDA.   O wonderful goose!

GILLIAN.   Great goose!

BELINDA.   Goose beyond compare!

PETER.   There! I've got it!

GILLIAN and MIRANDA.   Hurray! *(They grab Peter and then Belinda and dance around the table, chanting. Mrs. Cratchit smiles at them.)*

GILLIAN, MIRANDA, BELINDA and PETER.   *(Chanting.)*
>THE GOOSE, THE GOOSE, THE BEAUTIFUL
>   GOOSE!
>NOBODY HAS SUCH A GOOSE AS THIS!
>IT'S PLUMP AND IT'S TENDER AND IT'S HOT!
>O HOW PERFECT! O WHAT BLISS!

MRS. CRATCHIT.   Where's your precious father, then? And your bother, Tiny Tim? And Martha wasn't this late last Christmas!

BELINDA.   Here's Martha, mother! *(Enter Martha, also poor, about seventeen.)*

GILLIAN.   Here's Martha, mother!

PETER.   Hurray, Martha!

MIRANDA.   Martha! There's SUCH a goose!

MARTHA.   I can smell it! Belinda! Gillian! Miranda! Peter! *(Martha kisses her sisters and brother, then turns fondly toward her mother to embrace her.)*

SCROOGE.   Is it a very big goose, Spirit?

CHRISTMAS PRESENT.   No, it is very small. But they make the best of it.

MRS. CRATCHIT.   Bless your heart, my dear, how late you are!

MARTHA.   We had a lot of work we had to finish. They made us come in this morning, too.

SCROOGE.   Where does she work?

CHRISTMAS PRESENT.   In a mill.

MRS. CRATCHIT.   Never mind. So long as you're here. Get next to the fire, my dear, and get yourself warm!

PETER.   Here's father coming!

GILLIAN and MIRANDA. Hide! Hide! *(The children hide, throwing a threadbare blanket over themselves. Mrs. Cratchit works. Enter Bob Cratchit, his coat and long scarf covered with snow. On his shoulder is Tiny Tim, carrying his crutch, who is thin and pale. He has an iron brace attached to one leg. His right hand is withered.)*

SCROOGE. Who is that boy?

CHRISTMAS PRESENT. You will see.

SCROOGE. Is he sick?

CHRISTMAS PRESENT. In some ways yes, in other ways no.

SCROOGE. What do you mean by that?

CHRISTMAS PRESENT. You will see.

CRATCHIT. So? Where's our Martha?

MRS. CRATCHIT. Not coming.

CRATCHIT. Not coming? Really?

MRS. CRATCHIT. Absolutely not.

CRATCHIT. And Peter?

MRS. CRATCHIT. Not.

CRATCHIT. And Gillian?

MRS. CRATCHIT. Not.

CRATCHIT. And Belinda?

MRS. CRATCHIT. Not.

CRATCHIT. And Miranda?

MRS. CRATCHIT. Not, not, not, not, not coming.

TINY TIM. On Christmas Day? Where are they? *(Peter, Belinda, Gillian, Miranda and Martha throw off the blanket and jump up.)*

ALL. HERE WE ARE!

TINY TIM. Oh!

ALL. Hello, father! Hello, Tim! Tiny Tim!

SCROOGE. Tim? Is that his name?

CHRISTMAS PRESENT. They call him Tiny Tim.

SCROOGE. No wonder. He is very small, and pale.

TINY TIM. Hello! You should see the stars tonight! They're beautiful!

PETER. All right, Tim!

GILLIAN. Let's go see the stars!

TINY TIM. Let's go!

ALL. Let's go! *(Cratchit puts Tiny Tim down; he hobbles toward them. He trips, and falls sprawling.)*

SCROOGE.   He fell!

ALL.   OHH! TINY TIM!!

SCROOGE.   Help him up! Someone help him up! *(They rush to Tiny Tim, to help him stand up, but Tiny Tim holds out his hand, wanting to stand up by himself. His crutch is handed to him by Peter, who then steps back and lets Tiny Tim struggle to his feet again.)*

TINY TIM.   It's all right.

SCROOGE.   Stands up by himself, does he?

TINY TIM.   *(Taking crutch.)* Thank you.

SCROOGE.   Good!

TINY TIM.   *(Struggling to get up.)* Quite all right.

CHRISTMAS PRESENT.   You like that?

SCROOGE.   Yes!

CHRISTMAS PRESENT.   Why?

SCROOGE.   He has backbone! That's it! Get up by yourself, lad!

TINY TIM.   There!

SCROOGE.   There!

TINY TIM.   I'm fine now.

PETER.   Come along, Tim! *(Peter picks Tiny Tim up, and the others do too, putting him on Peter's shoulders. They all go off, Cratchit and his wife watching them. Then they look sadly at each other.)*

MRS. CRATCHIT.   How did our little Tim behave?

CRATCHIT.   As good as gold and better. He gets thoughtful not walking, sitting by himself so much. He thinks the strangest things you ever heard. *(Cratchit's children, Tiny Tim on their shoulders, gather outside in a group, moving almost as one person. They look up at the stars, which sparkle brightly.)*

CRATCHIT'S CHILDREN.   OOOOH! AHHHHHH! *(Cratchit's voice trembles.)*

CRATCHIT.   He told me, coming home, that he hoped people saw him in church, a cripple, because it might be pleasant for them to remember on Christmas Day, who made beggars walk and blind men see.

MRS. CRATCHIT.   Bless the boy.

CRATCHIT.   Yes. He's getting better! He's growing strong! And hearty!

MRS. CRATCHIT. Of course he is. *(Cratchit picks up Tiny Tim's crutch from off the floor and looks at it.)*

CRATCHIT'S CHILDREN. OOOOHH! AHHHHH!

SCROOGE. Spirit! Tiny Tim, did you say?

CHRISTMAS PRESENT. Tiny Tim, because he is thin —

SCROOGE. — and pale and small. I see that. What will happen to him?

CHRISTMAS PRESENT. It depends.

SCROOGE. On what?

CHRISTMAS PRESENT. It depends on you.

SCROOGE. What do you mean?

CHRISTMAS PRESENT. You will see.

SCROOGE. What's wrong with his hand?

CHRISTMAS PRESENT. It is withered.

SCROOGE. The iron brace?

CHRISTMAS PRESENT. His right leg. He can barely walk. *(Enter Tiny Tim, with the others.)*

TINY TIM. Oh, mother! The stars!

MARTHA. Just you wait!

PETER. It'll be the best Christmas ever! *(They put Tiny Tim on a stool by the fire.)*

BELINDA. Get warm, Tim.

TINY TIM. Thank you.

PETER. Now. Ready, Mother?

MRS. CRATCHIT. Ready! *(Music. A few mugs, one for every two Cratchits, are held out. Mrs. Cratchit takes a pot off the fire and pours hot cider into them.)*

ALL. Cider! Oooooooooh!

FEMALE CRATCHIT CHILDREN. It's hot!

MALE CRATCHIT CHILDREN. It's good! *(They drink their cider, sharing mugs.)*

SCROOGE. And not much else, I'll warrant. How big is their goose?

CHRISTMAS PRESENT. It is the size of one scrawny chicken.

SCROOGE. For all those hungry mouths. I knew it.

CHRISTMAS PRESENT. But what they have, they know how to share! Better, they know how to *enjoy* what they share! Look at them!

CRATCHIT. I propose a Merry Christmas to us all, my dears. God bless us!

ALL. God bless us!

TINY TIM. God bless us every one! *(The Cratchits drink their small mugs of cider.)*

SCROOGE. Spirit, that boy!

CHRISTMAS PRESENT. Yes?

SCROOGE. It seems to me that today I have seen many little boys. From the present and the past. But none so pale, so frail, as this one. Tell me if Tiny Tim will live.

CHRISTMAS PRESENT. I see a vacant chair in a poor chimney corner, and a crutch without an owner, carefully preserved. If these shadows remain unaltered by the future, the child will die.

SCROOGE. Oh, no, Spirit!

CHRISTMAS PRESENT. Oh, yes, Scrooge!

SCROOGE. Well, when? Ten years?

CHRISTMAS PRESENT. Sooner.

SCROOGE. Five?

CHRISTMAS PRESENT. Sooner!

SCROOGE. A year, a month, a week, WHAT?

CHRISTMAS PRESENT. What do you care? "If children have to die, why let them do it and decrease the surface population."

SCROOGE. Did I say that?

CHRISTMAS PRESENT. Yes! *(Scrooge bows his head in shame. Cratchit stands up.)*

CRATCHIT. I give you — Mr. Scrooge! The Founder of the Feast!

MRS. CRATCHIT. Mr. Scrooge? Founder of the Feast indeed!

CRATCHIT. My dear.

MRS. CRATCHIT. I wish I had him here, I'd give him something to feast on! A piece of my mind, that's what, and I hope he'd have a good appetite for it!

CRATCHIT. My dear, the children. Christmas Day.

MRS. CRATCHIT. It has to be Christmas to drink to the health of such an odious, stingy, hard, unfeeling man as Mr. Scrooge. You know he is, Robert. Nobody knows it better than you do, poor fellow. Well, I drink his health for your sake, and the Day's, not for his.

CRATCHIT. Thank you, my dear.

MRS. CRATCHIT. Long life to him. A merry Christmas and a Happy New Year, wherever he is, very merry and very happy, I'm sure!!

CRATCHIT. Mr. Scrooge.

TINY TIM. Mr. Scrooge!

ALL. *(Quietly.)* Mr. Scrooge.

SCROOGE. Ah! Spirit!

CHRISTMAS PRESENT. Who have you to blame but yourself?

CRATCHIT. Now then, a song, a song!

MARTHA. Tim, what'll it be?

TINY TIM. "The Little Boy Lost In The Snow."

ALL. THE LITTLE BOY LOST IN THE SNOW! *(Singing, perhaps as a round.)*

> A BOY DID GO OUT INTO THE SNOW,
> TO FIND HIS LITTLE SPOTTED DOG JOE.
>
> O LITTLE BOY LOST! O LITTLE BOY LOST!
> BRING HIM HOME WHATEVER THE COST!
> ON THIS ICY COLD CHRISTMAS DAY.
>
> HE CALLED AND HE CALLED INTO THE WIND,
> UNTIL ALL HIS LITTLE BREATH HE DID SPEND.
>
> O LITTLE BOY LOST! OH LITTLE BOY LOST!
> O BRING HIM HOME WHATEVER THE COST!
> ON THIS ICY COLD CHRISTMAS DAY.
>
> THEN JOE RAN TO HIM AND BEGAN TO BARK,
> AND SO THEY WERE FOUND ALL SAFE IN THE
>   DARK!

O LITTLE BOY FOUND! O LITTLE BOY FOUND!
BRING HIM HOME AND GATHER AROUND!
ON THIS ICY COLD CHRISTMAS DAY.

(They all gather around Tiny Tim and sing the last verse again, loudly and happily, as the Cratchit's hearth begins to move. Singing.)

O LITTLE BOY FOUND! O LITTLE BOY FOUND!
BRING HIM HOME AND GATHER AROUND!
ON THIS ICY COLD CHRISTMAS DAY!*

(As they all sing the last verse, the lights go down on them. Scrooge points at Tiny Tim.)

SCROOGE.   But that boy! Wait! That boy! *(The Cratchit hearth begins slowly to turn around. Light focuses on Scrooge and the Ghost of Christmas Present, D.)*

CHRISTMAS PRESENT.   Come! *(Wind. Against the back wall or on a screen, projections and films of etchings and paintings and living people of Victorian England celebrating Christmas, plus a sound montage of different carols, all rushed together with the wind. Light on the Ghost of Christmas Present, holding Scrooge around the shoulders and pointing ahead of them. We hear the voice of the Ghost of Christmas Present as we watch the scene change.)* Do you see, Scrooge! Christmas Present! People in the streets, in the fields, in the mines, in the cities and in the countries, on the land and on the sea, they stop. They have a kinder word for each other than at any other time of the year! This is my Spirit! The Spirit of Christmas! Good cheer, kindness, and love! And some of it, Scrooge, some of it lasts throughout the year! *(The projections and films vanish, and a single voice is heard, laughing. Scrooge and the Ghost of Christmas Present stand aside to watch. The Cratchit hearth has turned around now, replaced by colorful red and green curtains, against a large window. Snow is falling outside the window. A small elegant table and a lovely small Victorian sofa. What was drab and poor is now comfortable and tasteful. Scrooge's Nephew comes onto the stage, with a beautiful clear glass of ruby red port.)*

NEPHEW.   Ha, ha, ha, ha! He said that Christmas was — bah, humbug! And he believed it too! *(Behind him, also carrying glasses of red port, come Scrooge's Niece-in-law, her Sister, who is very pretty and very fetching, and behind her, a very healthy young man named Topper, eye fixed on the Sister.)*

* See Special Note on Songs and Recordings on copyright page.

NIECE.   The more shame on him!

NEPHEW.   He's a comical old fellow, my uncle, but to tell you the truth, not so pleasant as he could be. Nobody knows why. However, his offenses carry their own punishments. He can't be very happy.

SISTER.   Is he very rich, Fred?

NEPHEW.   Oh, I think so.

TOPPER.   I'll be rich someday.

SISTER.   But you're not now.

TOPPER.   But I will be.

SISTER.   Not so close, if you please.

NIECE.   Oh, I think Scrooge is rich, Fred. Very very rich!

NEPHEW.   What if he is, my dear? His money's no use to him because he doesn't know what to do with it. I couldn't be mad at him if I tried.

NIECE.   Well, I could. He's a mean old skinflint.

SCROOGE.   They don't like me.

CHRISTMAS PRESENT.   Did you expect them to?

SCROOGE.   No! Yes! I DON'T KNOW!

NIECE.   He says he doesn't like us. He won't come have dinner with us,

NEPHEW.   So he misses a wonderful dinner! You see what I mean!

SISTER.   What do you think, Topper?

TOPPER.   I am a miserable bachelor. I live alone, just like him. I sleep alone, too.

SISTER.   Now, now!

TOPPER.   Well, I do!! How can I say anything about Scrooge?

NIECE.   Quite so.

TOPPER.   But I wish I WAS married. I wish I DIDN'T sleep alone. *(To Sister, very close.)* How about YOU?

SISTER.   Oh!

NEPHEW.   Well, I am going to give him the same chance every year whether he likes it or not. He can always come to dinner here. I will always say Merry Christmas, Uncle Scrooge! How are you and how is your clerk, Bob Cratchit, and when are you going to give him a raise from that wretched penance you pay him!

CHRISTMAS PRESENT.   When are you?

SCROOGE.   Oh, well, I don't know about that.

CHRISTMAS PRESENT.   You're hopeless.

TOPPER.   Let's play a game! *(He puts his glass of port on the table.)* I love a good game!

NIECE.   What do you want to play, Topper?

TOPPER.   Oh, Blind Man's Bluff. Here! *(Topper quickly ties a kerchief around his eyes and holds out his arms. The others put their glasses of port on the table.)* Now, then! Wherereeree are you!! *(Topper lunges for the Sister, who squeals and jumps away. Nephew and Niece laugh and move out of the way.)* I'm getting close to YOUUUUUU!!!

SISTER.   Stop it!! *(A delighted squeal.)* Ohhhhhhh!

TOPPER.   Got you! *(Topper grabs the Sister.)* Do I get a kiss? Of course I do! *(Topper kisses the Sister.)*

SISTER.   And this with it! *(The Sister bops Topper with her fan. He takes off his kerchief and bows to her.)*

TOPPER.   It was worth it! Let's play another! *(He reaches for her again and she scoots out of his grasp.)*

NEPHEW.   Let's play Yes and No.

NIECE, SISTER, and TOPPER.   All right!

NEPHEW.   I am thinking of an animal.

NIECE.   Live?

NEPHEW.   Yes!

SISTER.   Lives in a menagerie?

NEPHEW.   No!

TOPPER.   Killed for a market?

NEPHEW.   No!

SISTER.   A horse?

NEPHEW.   No!

TOPPER.   An ass!

NEPHEW.   Not exactly!

NIECE.   Cow or bull?

NEPHEW.   No!

TOPPER.   Tiger?

NEPHEW.   No!

NIECE.   Dog?

NEPHEW.   No!

SISTER. Cat?

NEPHEW. No!

SISTER. Pig?

NEPHEW. No!

TOPPER. Bear?

NEPHEW. No!

NIECE. Agreeable?

NEPHEW. No!

TOPPER. DISagreeable?

NEPHEW. YES!

TOPPER. Savage!

NEPHEW. Yes!

TOPPER. Growls and grunts!

NEPHEW. Yes!

TOPPER. Lives in London!

NEPHEW. Yes!

TOPPER. Makes money!

ALL. YES!

SCROOGE. WHO IS IT?

TOPPER. It's Uncle Scrooge!

ALL. IT'S UNCLE SCROOGE! *(They laugh. Scrooge gets it, nods his head.)*

SCROOGE. Ah, of course. Very funny!

NEPHEW. Well, he's given us a laugh, finally. Here, let's take up our port, and wish a Merry Christmas and a Happy New Year to the old man, wherever he is!

SCROOGE. I'm HERE! Right HERE!

NEPHEW. He wouldn't wish it for us, but may he have it nevertheless! I give you — Uncle Scrooge!

ALL. UNCLE SCROOGE!!! *(They toast Scrooge. The window, table and sofa move away, with the Nephew and others, who go smiling, drinking, and talking. The quarter hour bell sounds. Wind again. Empty stage, with Scrooge and the Ghost of Christmas Present standing alone against a bleak winter sky.)*

SCROOGE. The bell! Are Spirit's lives so short?

CHRISTMAS PRESENT. My life upon this earth is very brief. It ends tonight.

SCROOGE. Tonight?

CHRISTMAS PRESENT.   Tonight. It is almost time. But before I go, look here. *(Behind the Ghost of Christmas Present, a trap has risen, with two small figures on it. The Ghost of Christmas Present holds out his arms and around him, under his arms, appears a small, ragged, utterly wretched, frightened Little Boy. He hangs onto the great robe of the Ghost of Christmas Present.)*

SCROOGE.   Oh, Spirit! Is he yours?

CHRISTMAS PRESENT.   No, he is yours, and so is she. *(An equally wan and dirty and ragged Little Girl comes around the other side of the Ghost of Christmas Present.)* They are Man's. And they cling to me, because they have no father or mother. The boy is Ignorance. The girl is Want. Beware them both, Scrooge, for in their faces I see your Doom.

SCROOGE.   Have they no refuge?

CHRISTMAS PRESENT.   ARE THERE NO PRISONS? ARE THERE NO WORKHOUSES? *(The Ghost of Christmas Present, the Little Boy and the Little Girl point at Scrooge and exit. The bell sounds once. Ominous music: perhaps just a sinister buzz. A single figure, enormous, rises, very slowly. It becomes, slowly, a gigantic black cloak-like figure that almost fills the back of the stage: a figure of all-conquering Death. Scrooge turns and sees it.)*

SCROOGE.   Oh! *(Scrooge drops to his knees, in terror. From this figure emerges another, smaller figure, the same but life size, in the same black robe. This is the Spirit of Christmas Yet to Come. Against the huge black figure, the smaller figure stands, not speaking, looking at Scrooge.)* Are you the Spirit of a Christmas Yet To Come? *(The Spirit nods.)* You are about to show me shadows of things that have not happened but will happen in the time before us? *(The Spirit points onward.)* Phantom of the Future. I fear you more than any specter I have seen. But as I know you propose to do me good, and as I hope to live to be another man from what I was, I am prepared to bear you company and do it with a thankful heart. Will you not speak to me? *(No response.)* Lead on, Spirit. *(Wind. The Spirit of Christmas Yet to Come moves away and Scrooge follows him. They meet a street corner, moving toward them, and stand by it. Sounds of busy London streets. Three Businessmen stroll on, crude versions of the Business-*

men in Act One.)

FIRST BUSINESSMAN.   I don't know much about it either way. I only know he's dead. *(Scrooge moves away from the Spirit of Christmas Yet to Come and listens to what they have to say.)*

SECOND BUSINESSMAN.   When did he go?

FIRST BUSINESSMAN.   Last night, I believe. *(The First Businessman takes a box of snuff and offers it around. They all take a pinch and put snuff on their wrists.)*

THIRD BUSINESSMAN.   I thought he'd never die. What was the matter with him?

FIRST BUSINESSMAN.   *(Yawning.)* God knows.

THIRD BUSINESSMAN.   What has he done with his money?

FIRST BUSINESSMAN.   Haven't heard.

SECOND BUSINESSMAN.   Left it to his Company, perhaps.

FIRST BUSINESSMAN.   He hasn't left it to ME. That's all I know! *(They laugh at that.)*

THIRD BUSINESSMAN.   It's likely to be a very cheap funeral, for upon my life, I don't know of anyone who would go to it.

SECOND BUSINESSMAN.   Shall we make up a party and volunteer to go?

FIRST BUSINESSMAN.   I don't mind going, if a lunch is provided. I never go to a funeral unless I get lunch. *(He holds out his wrist. They do, too. All three Businessmen sniff in the snuff, hold it a minute, and then all sneeze together, in one huge happy convulsion.)*

BUSINESSMEN.   Aaa-choooooo!!!!

FIRST BUSINESSMAN.   Ah, good!

SECOND BUSINESSMAN.   Very good!

THIRD BUSINESSMAN.   Very very good!

SCROOGE.   This is Christmas Yet to Come? Well, somebody died. I see that. But what does that have to do with me, Spirit? *(The Spirit of Christmas Yet to Come points again. Above them descends a third sign: RAGS & BONES. Three Old Hags rush on. Charwoman has white hair and a pale face. Laundress is roughed up, with red cheeks and livid lips. Undertaker's Woman is humpbacked. They are dressed in rags but colorfully so, carry old bundles of things, each possessing great energy and ferocity. They elbow each other fiercely getting into a line. Scrooge and the Spirit of Christmas Yet to Come watch them fight.)*

CHARWOMAN.   I'm first!

LAUNDRESS.   Not on your life, dearie!

UNDERTAKER'S WOMAN.   I'm a cripple, get out of my way!

LAUNDRESS.   No, you get out of mine!

CHARWOMAN.   Me, I tell you, ME!

UNDERTAKER'S WOMAN.   No, ME!

ALL THREE HAGS.   ME!! *(Enter Old Joe, and behind him, his Gophers, dirty ragamuffin children, pulling a large cart which holds Old Joe's ill gotten gains. Old Joe is outlandishly dressed but in thrown away and cast off clothes of finery: elegant worn out shirts with lace sleeves, striped pants, coat with ragged velvet collar, stove pipe hat, etc. He carries a huge sack. He has the wild eye of a madman. Old Joe comes harshly between the Hags.)*

OLD JOE.   My Lady Charwoman is last! My Lady Laundress is in the middle! My Lady Undertaker's Woman is first! One! Two! Three!

LAUNDRESS.   All right, all right!

UNDERTAKER'S WOMAN.   You don't have to talk so mean to us.

CHARWOMAN.   We're all doing the same thing! *(They get into a line. Old Joe steps out in front of them.)*

OLD JOE.   Now then! It *is* a holiday. Here. *(Old Joe hands a flask of brandy to the Charwoman.)* One swig. *(Charwoman gulps it down. Old Joe grabs it from her.)* One I said one! *(Old Joe gives it to the Laundress. She gulps it down and he grabs it again.)* That was *two!* *(Old Joe gives the flask to the Undertaker's Woman.)*

UNDERTAKER'S WOMAN.   No, thank you.

OLD JOE.   What?

UNDERTAKER'S WOMAN.   I'm an undertaker's woman. I don't drink.

LAUNDRESS.   Why not?

UNDERTAKER'S WOMAN.   Dead people walk around when I do.

OLD JOE.   Well, then. Merry Christmas! *(Old Joe takes a big drink.)*

ALL THREE HAGS.   Merry Christmas!

OLD JOE.   So what'd you get out of this one?

CHARWOMAN.   This old man? Plenty!

OLD JOE.   Before he was cold, I'll wager!

LAUNDRESS.   Before he was dead!

OLD JOE.   No!

ALL THREE HAGS.   YES!! *(They laugh.)*

LAUNDRESS.   Why pretend? We're all doing the same thing here!

UNDERTAKER'S WOMAN.   Everybody's got a right to take care of themselves!

CHARWOMAN.   HE always did!! *(The three Hags laugh.)*

UNDERTAKER'S WOMAN.   Who's the worst for a few little lost things here and there? Not the dead man!

LAUNDRESS.   If he'd a wanted to keep anything after he was dead, the mean old screw, why wasn't he natural about it when he was alive? He'd have somebody to look after him when Death struck him, instead of lying there gasping out his last, alone all by himself!

CHARWOMAN.   THAT'S the truest word ever spoken!

UNDERTAKER'S WOMAN.   Let it be a judgement on him!

OLD JOE.   Right you are, and that's enough! Let me see it!

UNDERTAKER'S WOMAN.   Here! *(She opens her bundle. Old Joe takes out a ragged little account book and a pencil.)* A pencil case, velvet inside. A pair of sleeve buttons. And a beautiful necktie brooch. There!

OLD JOE.   I'll take sixpence off your account, and not another, not if I'm to be boiled in oil.

UNDERTAKER'S WOMAN.   Oh, that hurts!! But all right! *(She dumps her stuff into Old Joe's sack.)*

OLD JOE.   Next!

LAUNDRESS.   Here. *(She opens her bundle.)* Sheets and towels, a pair of pants, two gorgeous tea spoons and one pair of sugar tongs, and two boots!

OLD JOE.   I always give ladies too much! That's how I ruin myself! Half a crown, and if you ask me for a penny more, I'll knock it in two!

LAUNDRESS.   You're killing me! But all right! *(She dumps her stuff into Old Joe's sack.)*

OLD JOE.   Next!

CHARWOMAN.   Here's mine! *(She undoes a very large bundle.)* See?

OLD JOE.   What's all this?

CHARWOMAN.   Bed curtains!!

OLD JOE.   Oh, my sainted mother! You don't mean to say you took 'em down, rings and all, with him lying there?

CHARWOMAN.   I did so, and why not? What was he to do about it? *(Pause. Old Joe shakes his head.)*

OLD JOE.   Terrible! H'awful! SHAMEFUL! *(Laughs.)* Hee, hee, hee!! *(They all laugh.)* You were born to make your fortune and you'll let nothing stop you. What's this?

CHARWOMAN.   The finest nightshirt you ever seen. Not a hole in it. Been wasted, but for me.

OLD JOE.   What do you mean, wasted?

CHARWOMAN.   Why some fool put it on him to be buried in! I took it off his body and left him under a little calico and a sheet.

LAUNDRESS.   Quite becoming!

CHARWOMAN.   Well, he couldn't look any uglier than he did in this! *(They all laugh.)*

OLD JOE.   One pound for the lot!

CHARWOMAN.   AHHH!

OLD JOE.   Or you can take it home and wear it yourself!

CHARWOMAN.   This is worse than Death but ALL RIGHT! *(She stuffs everything of hers into the sack.)*

OLD JOE.   Ladies, I thank you!! *(Exeunt Old Joe, his Ragamuffins and the Three Hags.)*

SCROOGE.   Spirit, I own things like that. This poor man so robbed of everything, who was he? *(The Spirit of Christmas Yet to Come points. Wind, quietly. Lights go down. The stage is almost dark. Scrooge's own bed, but now without the curtains, bare, slides onto the stage. On it, under a sheet, lies a man's body.)* Merciful heaven, what is this? *(A pale light falls on the bed and the body. Scrooge recoils in horror from the body on the bed. He looks at the Spirit of Christmas Yet to Come, who points sternly toward the bed. Scrooge squares his shoulders, and forces himself to approach the body. He reaches out one hand and starts to lift the sheet from the dead man's face. Then stops. Scrooge looks at the Spirit of Christmas Yet to Come, who points at the sheet. Scrooge continues to lift the sheet from the dead man's face, stops.)* Is it *me? (He tries again, stops.)* Spirit, I would look if I could, but I can't! I will not forget this lesson! Trust me! Let us go from this awful place! Take me — take me to someone, anyone in all of London, who feels some emotion caused by this man's death! Can you do that? *(The Spirit of Christmas Yet to Come nods.)* Show me that person, Spirit, I beseech you! *(The Spirit of Christmas Yet to Come holds up his black cloak over Scrooge. Wind. The bed slides off. On the other side of the stage a young woman, Caroline, enters, pacing, worried. Three young Children stand frightened to one side, watching her. Her Husband comes to her, quickly.)*

CAROLINE.   The news! Is it good or bad?

HUSBAND.   Bad.

CAROLINE.   We are quite ruined?

HUSBAND.   No. There is some hope yet.

CAROLINE.   If he relents there is, but that would be a miracle!

HUSBAND.   He is past relenting now. He is dead.

CAROLINE.   Oh! *(She clasps her hands together, paces.)* I pray God's forgiveness! He was a human being and I am sorry, but I am glad to hear it! To whom will our debt be transferred?

HUSBAND.   I don't know. But before that time, perhaps we can be ready with the money we owe him.

CAROLINE.   And perhaps not.

HUSBAND.   Yes, but no other creditor can be as merciless as he!

CAROLINE.   You are right. No one!

HUSBAND.   So, because he's dead, we have some hope!
(Caroline and her Husband go to their Children and take them off-stage.)

SCROOGE.   Well, Spirit, yes, that *is* an emotion, but not what I had hoped for. They want me dead! Please, please let me see some tenderness here, not this eternal relentless hardness! Spirit, some tenderness, somewhere, please! *(The Spirit of Christmas Yet to Come raises his cloak again. Wind. Scrooge and the Spirit of Christmas Yet to Come move to one side. Now a second, smaller, poorer bed moves across the stage on a platform. The bed is empty. Sitting in a chair beside the bed, at its head, is Bob Cratchit. At the foot of the bed stand Mrs. Cratchit and all the Cratchit Children. Cratchit is reading from the Bible.)*

CRATCHIT.   "And he took a child and set him in the midst of them." *(He stops reading.)* My eyes hurt.

MRS. CRATCHIT.   You went again, Robert?

CRATCHIT.   Yes, my dear. I wish you all could have gone. It would have done you good to see how green a place it is. I promised him I would walk there every Sunday. *(He weeps.)* My child. My Tim.

SCROOGE.   Spirit, no! No!

CRATCHIT.   At the grave I met Mr. Scrooge's nephew, the pleasantest spoken gentleman you've ever heard. He said, "I am heartily sorry, Mr. Cratchit, for you and for your good wife and for your other children." He gave me his card. "If I can be of any service to you, in any way, please let me know." He was so kind. It was as if he had known our Tiny Tim himself.

MRS. CRATCHIT.   I'm sure he's a good soul.

CRATCHIT.   He said he might find Peter there a better situation, working for him.

MRS. CRATCHIT.   Hear that, Peter?

MIRANDA.   And then Peter will find himself a girl and set up house for himself.

PETER.   Get along.

CRATCHIT.   In time you will. You will part from us. But however and whenever we part from one another, I am sure we will never forget Tiny Tim, for his was the first parting there was among us.

MRS. CRATCHIT.   No, Bob.

CHILDREN.   Never, father.

CRATCHIT.   And I know, my dear, that when we remember how patient and how kind our Tim was, we shall not quarrel easily among ourselves and forget him in doing so.

CHILDREN.   No, father, never.

CRATCHIT.   Then, I am happy. I am very happy. *(He weeps.*

His family gathers around him as he sets the brace and the crutch down on the bed to embrace them. The bed, platform and Cratchits move away, leaving Scrooge alone, staring at the Spirit of Christmas Yet to Come. It is at this point that Scrooge begins to understand what has happened to him. What comes next is not a surprise to him. Toward Scrooge moves a grave, like Marley's grave at the beginning of the play.)

SCROOGE.   Before I draw nearer to this grave, answer me one question, Spirit. Are these the shadows of Things That Must Be or are they shadows of Things that May Be Only? Answer me! *(The Spirit of Christmas Yet to Come moves back into the great black shadow that has loomed above everything, pointing as he goes, and disappears. Scrooge goes to the grave. He kneels and brushes dirt away from its level, brass headstone. Reads.)* Scrooge. *(He stands up.)* Oh, Spirits, wherever you be, hear me! I am not the man I was! I will not be the man I have been! Why can I not change what you have shown me? *(Scrooge turns and faces the huge black figure behind him. Light glows behind it, making it an even more formidable presence.)* Why show me all this if I am past all hope? *(A crashing dissonant chord. Scrooge runs to the figure, seizes its cloth substance and pulls the whole great thing down to the floor. It parts in the middle. Each side is whipped offstage and is gone. Blackout! Sound: tremendous noise, reverberating! Lights whirl around the proscenium! Every possible effect! Silence. As the reverberations die away, slow light discovers Scrooge, eyes closed, holding on to one of the bedposts of his bed, which sits alone now on the stage, backed by a wintry sky.)* Spirit! Spirit! I will honor Christmas in my heart and try to keep it all year! I will live in the Past, the Present and the Future! I will not shut out the lessons you have taught me! Spirit! *(Pause.)* Ah! Where am I now? A bedpost. *My* bedpost! My curtains, not torn down! Am I home again, with everything just as it was, my bed, my room, my house! No. It's different. I'm different. But how? I don't know, exactly, but I am. How long was I among the Spirits? I don't know. I don't know anything. I don't *have* to know anything. I'm just a baby, a child again! Newborn, me?? Scrooge??? Never mind. Good. I don't care! I'll *be* a child! *(D. below Scrooge and his bed, the Boy who sings the carol appears in a spotlight.)*

BOY. *(Singing.)*
NOEL, NOEL.
NOEL, NOEL.
BORN IS A CHILD IN ISRAEL.
SCROOGE. Hallo there! You! You there!
BOY. Wot? *(Scrooge reaches into the curtains of the bed and pulls out his long overcoat, his scarf and a cap.)*
SCROOGE. My fine fellow!
BOY. Yis?
SCROOGE. My boy!
BOY. Yis? *(Scrooge goes to the Boy, dressed in coat, scarf, cap, but still wearing his slippers and nightshirt underneath.)*
SCROOGE. What's today?
BOY. Today? It's Christmas day. Ye daft?
SCROOGE. It's Christmas Day! I haven't missed it! They did it all in one night! Of course they did. Spirits can do anything they like!
BOY. Wot?
SCROOGE. They did! Do you hear me?
BOY. Yis, yis, I hear you!
SCROOGE. Now then, my boy!
BOY. Yis?
SCROOGE. Do you know the poulterer's, in the next street but one, at the corner?
BOY. I should hope I do!
SCROOGE. Intelligent boy. Remarkable boy. Do you know if they've sold the prize turkey that was hanging in the window? Not the little prize turkey! I mean the great big enormous one!
BOY. Wot, the one big as me?
SCROOGE. What a delightful boy. It's a pleasure to talk to him. Yes, my lad!
BOY. It's 'anging there now!
SCROOGE. Go and buy it!
BOY. Not bloody likely!!
SCROOGE. No, no! I'm in earnest! Money! See?
BOY. Oooooooo!

SCROOGE. I put it in this pouch. Go buy the turkey. Then take it, IN A CAB —

BOY. Ina CAB, Ooooooo!

SCROOGE. To Camden Town, to the little house of Robert Cratchit. If he's not at home, find out where he is. Give him the turkey. And keep the rest of the money for yourself Can you do that?

BOY. Bloody likely, Guv!!! *(Scrooge slaps the pouch in his hand.)*

SCROOGE. Run, as I used to run, when I was you! Run!

BOY. I'm off!!!! *(The Boy dashes off. Scrooge thinks, takes stock of himself. He is feeling a new, slow, blossoming feeling: happiness.)*

SCROOGE. Bob Cratchit won't know who sent it! Hee hee! *(Suddenly, Scrooge stops himself.)* What am I doing? This isn't me! Is it? I feel very strange. I'm not used to being — this way. Can I do this? Yes, I can! And I'll get better at it! I will! *(Pause. He thinks of something very funny.)* Ha ha! That turkey! It's the size — it's TWICE the size of Tiny Tim! Ha ha! *(Stops, thinks.)* Tiny Tim. Is the boy still alive? I am still alive. If the boy in me is still alive, so Tiny Tim must be alive, too. Yes! That's it! I'm off, like a shot! *(Wind. Scrooge's bed and room move off. A confusion of street voices and muffled carols in a sound montage. The colors on the proscenium begin to glow again and light up. A slow procession of Christmas decorations begins now to descend, reaching, only at the end of the play, the spectacle of a huge cornucopia of trees, presents, wreaths, food, and everything good about Christmas, hanging before us against a shy turning a beautiful deep blue. Carols, very low at first, begin to be heard. The streets. Enter to one upper corner of the stage, Gentleman I and Gentleman 2. Scrooge rushes past them.)*

GENTLEMAN 1. Who was that?

GENTLEMAN 2. Scrooge.

GENTLEMAN 1. Oh, dear. *(Scrooge runs back to them.)*

SCROOGE. Gentlemen, gentleman, how do you do? *(He takes both men by the hand.)* I hope you succeeded in your fund raising for the poor yesterday. Merry Christmas to you both!

GENTLEMAN 1. *(Surprised.)* Mr. Scrooge?

GENTLEMAN 2. *(Equally so.)* Mr. Scrooge?

SCROOGE. That's my name, not very pleasant to hear. Let me change that. First, I beg your pardon for my neglect of your cause. Second, will you allow me to donate — *(He whispers in their ears. Their faces brighten.)*

GENTLEMAN 1. Why, Mr. Scrooge!

GENTLEMAN 2. Are you serious?

SCROOGE. Not a farthing less! Includes a great many back payments, you see! *(They pump his hand.)*

GENTLEMAN 1. Thank you, sir!

GENTLEMAN 2. We don't know what to say!

SCROOGE. Don't say anything. Just come and see me, about future contributions! Will you do that?

GENTLEMAN 1 and 2. WE WILL!!

SCROOGE. Thankee! Much obliged! Bless you. I'm off! *(Exeunt Gentlemen 1 and 2 and Scrooge. Enter to another upper corner of the stage, Caroline and Husband. Enter Scrooge.)* Ah-ha! You two!

HUSBAND. Oh, my God.

CAROLINE. Scrooge!

SCROOGE. Don't try to run away! You owe me money! A lot of money! See that you pay it! Some day. Ha ha! Some day soon. Ha ha! Or some day not so soon! Ha ha ha! As a matter of fact, come to my office tomorrow and we'll tear up that contract and make another. Or just tear up that contract! Ha ha! Merry Christmas! God bless you! *(Scrooge kisses both heartily on the cheek.)* Yes! I can do this! *(Scrooge dashes off. Caroline and Husband stare at each other, and exit. Enter Nephew and Niece, to a lower corner of the stage. Enter Scrooge.)* Fred!

NEPHEW. Uncle?

SCROOGE. Merry Christmas, Fred. May I come to dinner?

NIECE. May you what?

SCROOGE. If you can stand me.

NEPHEW. On one condition.

SCROOGE. What's that?

NEPHEW. That it be not just this Christmas, but all the rest. Dinner with your family on Christmas Day, Uncle!

SCROOGE. With all my heart!

NEPHEW.   Then come with us now!

SCROOGE.   I'll be there tonight. Now, there is one other place I must go.

NIECE.   Then we'll see you at dinner!

SCROOGE.   Dinner! Ha! I'm getting *very* good at this!! *(Exit Scrooge, running.)*

NIECE.   I don't believe it!

NEPHEW.   Neither do I! *(Exeunt Nephew and Niece. The mix of carols grows louder. Lights grow brighter. A part of the Cratchit family home. They are all gathered around an enormous turkey. Scrooge appears and confronts them, scowling.)*

SCROOGE.   Now then, Cratchits! Where did you get that turkey?

MIRANDA.   We don't know!

GILLIAN.   It just came.

MIRANDA.   A strange boy brought it.

SCROOGE.   It's big enough. You'll eat it all and you'll oversleep and be late to work, Bob Cratchit!

CRATCHIT.   No, Mr. Scrooge.

SCROOGE.   Don't contradict me!

CRATCHIT.   No, Mr. Scrooge!

SCROOGE.   Let me tell you this, Bob Cratchit. I am not going to stand for this sort of behavior one minute longer. And therefore —

CRATCHIT.   Oh, Mr. Scrooge!

SCROOGE.   And therefore, I am about to raise your salary!

CRATCHITS.   What????

SCROOGE.   *(Gesture.)* Take that! Raise! Yes, raise! You know? Up, up!

CRATCHITS.   What????

SCROOGE.   A Merry Christmas, Bob. A merrier Christmas than I have ever given you. I'll raise your salary and endeavor to help you and your family and oh, Tiny Tim. *(Scrooge steps back, putting as much distance between him and the Cratchits as possible.)* I am almost afraid to ask. Is Tiny Tim here? *(Tiny Tim, who had been hiding behind his brother and sisters, with his crutch limps forward.)*

MRS. CRATCHIT.   Tim.

CRATCHIT.   Say hello to Mr. Scrooge. *(Tiny Tim limps a little further out by himself. Lights down on the others. Scrooge and Tiny Tim face each other, brightly lit.)*

TINY TIM.   Hello, sir.

SCROOGE.   How are you, my boy?

TINY TIM.   All right, sir.

SCROOGE.   Quite lively, in fact?

TINY TIM.   Oh, yes, sir.

SCROOGE.   Would you, if your father permits, spend some time with an old man?

TINY TIM.   If the old man was you, yes, sir, I would.

SCROOGE.   We might see about that brace, and what can be done to make a better one.

TINY TIM.   Thank you, sir.

SCROOGE.   Ebenezer.

TINY TIM.   Ebenezer.

SCROOGE.   That's it.

TINY TIM.   But — Ebenezer —

SCROOGE.   Yes, Tim?

TINY TIM.   Why are you being so nice to me?

SCROOGE.   Because, because, if you are alive, my dear boy, then so am I. *(Tiny Tim hobbles toward Scrooge, Scrooge runs toward him. Tiny Tim runs into Scrooge's arms.)*

VOICE.   Scrooge was better than his word. To Tiny Tim he became a second father, and to the family and to the city of London as good a friend as it ever knew. Some people laughed to see the change in him, but in his own heart, Scrooge was laughing too, like a boy, and that was enough for him. *(Crashing full orchestra, and everyone singing:)*

ALL.
>   NOEL, NOEL!
>   NOEL, NOEL!
>   BORN IS A CHILD IN ISRAEL!

(The sky is beautiful, the hanging Christmas decorations are beautiful. All gather around and sing the carol, watching Scrooge and Tiny Tim, who sit down together on the stage in a spotlight, while Scrooge

tells Tiny Tim stories. Then Scrooge stands up and sweeps Tiny Tim up, onto his shoulders.)

TINY TIM.   God bless us, every one!

SCROOGE.   God bless us, every one!

ALL.   *(To the audience.)* God bless us, every one! *(Music. Lights build to a great brightness. Scrooge, Tiny Tim and ALL wave to the audience.)*

CURTAIN

POSSIBLE CAST BREAKDOWN

MEN

SCROOGE
BOB CRATCHIT

Company
Ages: 20–30 (3); 30–40 (3); 50 (1)

NEPHEW, CHRISTMAS YET TO COME
GENTLEMAN 1, BUSINESSMAN 1
SCROOGE YOUNG, HUSBAND
CHRISTMAS PAST, GENTLEMAN 2, BUSINESSMAN 2
FEZZIWIG, OLD MAN, OLD JOE, MARLEY
TOPPER, MAN, COUPLE
CHRISTMAS PRESENT, BUSINESSMAN 3
YOUNG FATHER

TOTAL: 6 men plus Scrooge & Cratchit = 9 MEN

WOMEN

Company
Ages: 20–30 (3); 50 (1)

FAN, NIECE, UNDERTAKER'S WOMAN
MRS. FEZZIWIG, CHARWOMAN
BELLE, MARTHA, SISTER, LAUNDRESS
MRS. CRATCHIT, THREADBARE WOMAN
YOUNG MOTHER

TOTAL: 4 women

CHILDREN
May be multiple cast or not

TINY TIM
CAROL BOY

Company
BOY 1, MISERABLE CHILD BOY
BOY 2
BOY 3
SCROOGE AS BOY
FEZZIWIG DAUGHTER 1, MELINDA, MISERABLE
      CHILD GIRL
FEZZIWIG DAUGHTER 2, BELINDA
FEZZIWIG DAUGHTER 3, GILLIAN

CHILDREN: as few as 6 boys and 3 girls = 9 children
TOTAL COMPANY — 9 men, 4 women, 9 children
(13 adult actors, 9 children)

TOTAL COMPANY OF 22 actors

SIMPLER ALTERNATE VERSION OF:

A CHRISTMAS CAROL

CHARACTERS

EBENEZER SCROOGE
A NAMELESS BOY
BOB CRATCHIT
TINY TIME
THE COMPANY:
MEN, WOMEN and CHILDREN OF LONDON

TIME

Awhile ago

PLACE

London, England

SIMPLER ALTERNATE VERSION OF:

A CHRISTMAS CAROL

A simple stage or a room is a bright, warm and friendly place.

At center, several chairs with brocaded seats. Leaning against them, whatever musical instruments the actors can manage: violin, bass fiddle, guitar, flute, drums, kazoo, ukulele, tambourine, whatever can be played. Wind is made by a small wind machine or by actors making noise. This may all be enhanced by music on tape.

While the audience is being seated, one Company member comes on, takes up an instrument, plays on it a bit. Then another, saying hello to the first, does the same. Then another, who sits at the piano and begins to play an old English carol. The first to enter sings the words, the second plays an instrument.

As the audience is being seated, the rest of the Company comes on, singly, two by two, three by three, etc., and join in. They all either play an instrument or sing, and by curtain time, the whole Company is onstage, happily singing carols to themselves.

A large bell tolls three times. Company keeps playing and singing.

Lights change.

Sound of a harsh cold wind, very low, is created. It shrieks, then dies down to a low howl. Singing and wind continue.

The Company finishes its last carol.

The actor who will play the Nephew, addresses the others.

NEPHEW.   Once Upon a Time — Marley was dead!
OTHERS.   *(Unison.)* Dead!
NEPHEW.   There was no doubt about it!
OTHERS.   *(Unison.)* Dead, dead, dead!!
NEPHEW.   Did Scrooge know he was dead?
OTHERS.   *(Unison.)* Yes!!
NEPHEW.   This must be distinctly understood!
OTHERS.   *(Unison.)* Distinctly! *(They all get up and start moving things about: chairs go against walls, crates are stacked to create desks, and so on. Someone places a sign somewhere that says SCROOGE & MARLEY. Bob Cratchit, with his long scarf and threadbare coat, trudges along imaginary streets to the office, enters it and lights a candle inside.)*
NEPHEW.   Otherwise nothing wonderful can come of the story we are about to relate.
OTHERS.   Nothing!!
NEPHEW.   For Scrooge never painted out old Marley's name! There it hung on the sign above the warehouse door: Scrooge & Marley!
OTHERS.   Scrooge & Marley!!
NEPHEW.   And on this particular Christmas Eve, in cold, bleak, biting weather —
OTHERS.   *(Unison.)* Old Scrooge came to his counting house! *(Enter Scrooge. He holds his hat with one hand, his cane with the other, his ledger book under one arm.)*
NEPHEW.   Oh, he was tight-fisted!! Squeezing —
OTHERS.   *(Unison.)* Wrenching!
NEPHEW.   Grasping!
OTHERS.   *(Unison.)* Scraping!
NEPHEW.   Clutching!
OTHERS.   *(Unison.)* Ebenezer Scrooge! *(Scrooge is confronted by a Boy, perhaps Tiny Tim, who is in his way, and doesn't know how to get out of it. Scrooge stares at him a second, then brushes him out*

of his way with his cane, continues on, with the Boy staring after him, then running off. Scrooge stops and turns, and looks after the Boy, puzzled by something. He doesn't know what it is. He moves on toward his office.)

NEPHEW.   No warmth could warm him. No cold could chill him. He was as hard and as sharp as flint!

OTHERS.   As flint!!

NEPHEW.   But now, fighting through the fog and the cold and the driven snow, old Scrooge felt that something, he knew not what, was wrong, very wrong, on this particular day. *(Scrooge stops before his office door, and looks about, puzzled again, very uneasy.)* But he decided it was only Christmas Eve!

SCROOGE.   Bah! Humbug! *(Scrooge goes into his office, by the sign SCROOGE & MARLEY.)*

OTHERS.   *(Unison.)* And into his counting house he goes! *(Scrooge lights a candle on his desk, opens his ledger book, and begins to work, muttering as he works. A second candle is lit, and we see Bob Cratchit, silently working at a smaller desk with a smaller candle.)*

SCROOGE.   Rent! Interest! Dividend! Penalty! Semi-annually!

NEPHEW.   People go wheezing as they struggle up and down the streets all day long, beating their hands on their chests and stamping their feet. *(Clocks strike three.)* The city clocks had only struck three, but it got dark. Oh! How dark it was, how damp it was, how the cold wind blew!

OTHERS.   *(Offstage, unison.)* And old Scrooge sat in his counting house!!

SCROOGE.   *(To himself, working.)* Bah. *(He works.)* Humbug. *(Scrooge is a lean, sardonic old man, with a hard ice cold secret life. Bob Cratchit is a friendly outgoing gentleman of large family and meager means. Enter Nephew.)*

NEPHEW.   Merry Christmas Uncle!

(The play now continues as written in the first version, with all its stage effects reduced to absolute simplicity: ghosts come in and out of one door, streets and houses and furniture are created from boxes, benches, chairs and crates. The ending:)

SCROOGE.   Ebenezer.

TINY TIM.   Ebenezer.

SCROOGE. That's it.

TINY TIM. But — Ebenezer —

SCROOGE. Yes, Tim?

TINY TIM. Why are you being so nice to me?

SCROOGE. Because, if you are alive, my dear boy, so am I.

TINY TIM. Oh! (*Tiny Tim runs into Scrooge's arms. The Company as seen at the beginning of the play comes on singing "Noel, Noel." They take up their same positions, except now, in front of them while they sing, are Scrooge and Tiny Tim. Scrooge and Tiny Tim sit down together on the stage, and Scrooge tells Tiny Tim stories. Then Scrooge stands up and sweeps Tiny Tim up, onto his shoulders. While this is happening:*)

NEPHEW. And my Uncle Scrooge was better than his word. He did it all and more. To Tiny Tim he became a second father, and to the family and to the city of London as good a friend as it ever knew. Some people laughed to see the change in him, but in his own heart, Scrooge was laughing too, like a boy, and that was enough for him.

TINY TIM. God bless us, every one!

SCROOGE. God bless us, every one!

ALL. (*To the audience.*) God bless us, every one! (*Scrooge and Tiny Tim wave to the audience. End of play. The actors smile, bow, and perhaps go shake hands and talk with the audience.*)

WOMEN
Ages: 20–30 (3); 50 (1)

FAN, NIECE, UNDERTAKER'S WOMAN
MRS. FEZZIWIG, CHARWOMAN
BELLE, MARTHA, SISTER, LAUNDRESS
MRS. CRATCHIT, THREADBARE WOMAN

TOTAL: 4 women

MEN
May be multiple cast or not

TINY TIM
CAROL BOY

COMPANY

BOY 1, MISERABLE CHILD BOY
BOY 2
BOY 3
SCROOGE AS BOY
FEZZIWIG DAUGHTER 1, MELINDA, MISERABLE
    CHILD GIRL
FEZZIWIG DAUGHTER 2, BELINDA
FEZZIWIG DAUGHTER 3, GILLIAN

CHILDREN: as few as 6 boys and 3 girls = 9 children

TOTAL COMPANY — 9 men, 4 women, 9 children (13 adult actors, 9 children)

TOTAL COMPANY of 22 actors

PROPERTY PLOT

ACT ONE

Walking cane (SCROOGE)
Papers (CRATCHIT)
Books, papers and pen (PORTLY GENTLEMEN 1 & 2)
Candles, matches (SCROOGE, CRATCHIT)
Ruler (SCROOGE)
Overcoat (SCROOGE)
Comforter (CRATCHIT)
Ledger book (SCROOGE)
Door key (SCROOGE)
Night shirt and cap (SCROOGE)
Bell pull (SCROOGE)
Book (SCROOGE AS A YOUNG BOY)
Papers (SCROOGE AS A YOUNG MAN)
Pocket watch (FEZZIWIG)

ACT TWO

Holly, mistletoe, ivy (draped)
Sausages on strings
Mince pies
Red apples
Oranges
Cakes
Plumb pudding
Small mirrors
Soiled clothes and sheets
Crutch (TINY TIM)
Leg brace (TINY TIM)
Mugs (CRATCHIT FAMILY)
Pot with cider (MRS. CRATCHIT)

Glasses of port wine (NEPHEW, NIECE, SISTER, TOPPER)
Handkerchief (TOPPER)
Fan (SISTER)
Box of snuff (FIRST BUSINESSMAN)
Old bundles (3 HAGS)
Large cart with items (GOPHER)
Huge sack (OLD JOE)
Flask of brandy (OLD JOE)
Account book, distressed (OLD JOE)
Pencil (OLD JOE)
Overcoat, scarf and hat (SCROOGE)
Pouch of money (SCROOGE)
Large turkey (CRATCHITS)
Christmas decorations

SOUND EFFECTS

Wind
Thunder
Howling wind
Bell tolling
Chains
Street sounds
Muffled voices
Muffled singing of carols
Mix of Christmas carols, sung clearly

NEW PLAYS

★ **A LESSON BEFORE DYING by Romulus Linney, based on the novel by Ernest J. Gaines.** An innocent young man is condemned to death in backwoods Louisiana and must learn to die with dignity. "The story's wrenching power lies not in its outrage but in the almost inexplicable grace the characters must muster as their only resistance to being treated like lesser beings." *—The New Yorker.* "Irresistable momentum and a cathartic explosion...a powerful inevitability." *—NY Times.* [5M, 2W] ISBN: 0-8222-1785-6

★ **BOOM TOWN by Jeff Daniels.** A searing drama mixing small-town love, politics and the consequences of betrayal. "...a brutally honest, contemporary foray into classic themes, exploring what moves people to lie, cheat, love and dream. By BOOM TOWN's climactic end there are no secrets, only bare truth." *—Oakland Press.* "...some of the most electrifying writing Daniels has ever done..." *—Ann Arbor News.* [2M, 1W] ISBN: 0-8222-1760-0

★ **INCORRUPTIBLE by Michael Hollinger.** When a motley order of medieval monks learns their patron saint no longer works miracles, a larcenous, one-eyed minstrel shows them an outrageous new way to pay old debts. "A lightning-fast farce, rich in both verbal and physical humor." *—American Theatre.* "Everything fits snugly in this funny, endearing black comedy...an artful blend of the mock-formal and the anachronistically breezy...A piece of remarkably dexterous craftsmanship." *—Philadelphia Inquirer.* "A farcical romp, scintillating and irreverent." *—Philadelphia Weekly.* [5M, 3W] ISBN: 0-8222-1787-2

★ **CELLINI by John Patrick Shanley.** Chronicles the life of the original "Renaissance Man," Benvenuto Cellini, the sixteenth-century Italian sculptor and man-about-town. Adapted from the autobiography of Benvenuto Cellini, translated by J. Addington Symonds. "[Shanley] has created a convincing Cellini, not neglecting his dark side, and a trim, vigorous, fast-moving show." *—BackStage.* "Very entertaining...With brave purpose, the narrative undermines chronology before untangling it...touching and funny..." *—NY Times.* [7M, 2W (doubling)] ISBN: 0-8222-1808-9

★ **PRAYING FOR RAIN by Robert Vaughan.** Examines a burst of fatal violence and its aftermath in a suburban high school. "Thought provoking and compelling." *—Denver Post.* "Vaughan's powerful drama offers hope and possibilities." *—Theatre.com.* "[The play] doesn't put forth compact, tidy answers to the problem of youth violence. What it does offer is a compelling exploration of the forces that influence an individual's choices, and of the proverbial lifelines—be they familial, communal, religious or political—that tragically slacken when society gives in to apathy, fear and self-doubt..." *—Westword.* "...a symphony of anger..." *—Gazette Telegraph.* [4M, 3W] ISBN: 0-8222-1807-0

★ **GOD'S MAN IN TEXAS by David Rambo.** When a young pastor takes over one of the most prestigious Baptist churches from a rip-roaring old preacher-entrepreneur, all hell breaks loose. "...the pick of the litter of all the works at the Humana Festival..." *—Providence Journal.* "...a wealth of both drama and comedy in the struggle for power..." *—LA Times.* "...the first act is so funny...deepens in the second act into a sobering portrait of fear, hope and self-delusion..." *—Columbus Dispatch.* [3M] ISBN: 0-8222-1801-1

★ **JESUS HOPPED THE 'A' TRAIN by Stephen Adly Guirgis.** A probing, intense portrait of lives behind bars at Rikers Island. "...fire-breathing...whenever it appears that JESUS is settling into familiar territory, it slides right beneath expectations into another, fresher direction. It has the courage of its intellectual restlessness...[JESUS HOPPED THE 'A' TRAIN] has been written in flame." *—NY Times.* [4M, 1W] ISBN: 0-8222-1799-6

DRAMATISTS PLAY SERVICE, INC.
440 Park Avenue South, New York, NY 10016 212-683-8960 Fax 212-213-1539
postmaster@dramatists.com www.dramatists.com

NEW PLAYS

★ **THE CIDER HOUSE RULES, PARTS 1 & 2 by Peter Parnell, adapted from the novel by John Irving.** Spanning eight decades of American life, this adaptation from the Irving novel tells the story of Dr. Wilbur Larch, founder of the St. Cloud's, Maine orphanage and hospital, and of the complex father-son relationship he develops with the young orphan Homer Wells. "...luxurious digressions, confident pacing...an enterprise of scope and vigor..." *–NY Times.* "...The fact that I can't wait to see Part 2 only begins to suggest just how good it is..." *–NY Daily News.* "...engrossing...an odyssey that has only one major shortcoming: It comes to an end." *–Seattle Times.* "...outstanding...captures the humor, the humility...of Irving's 588-page novel..." *–Seattle Post-Intelligencer.* [9M, 10W, doubling, flexible casting] PART 1 ISBN: 0-8222-1725-2 PART 2 ISBN: 0-8222-1726-0

★ **TEN UNKNOWNS by Jon Robin Baitz.** An iconoclastic American painter in his seventies has his life turned upside down by an art dealer and his ex-boyfriend. "...breadth and complexity...a sweet and delicate harmony rises from the four cast members...Mr. Baitz is without peer among his contemporaries in creating dialogue that spontaneously conveys a character's social context and moral limitations..." *–NY Times.* "...darkly funny, brilliantly desperate comedy...TEN UNKNOWNS vibrates with vital voices." *–NY Post.* [3M, 1W] ISBN: 0-8222-1826-7

★ **BOOK OF DAYS by Lanford Wilson.** A small-town actress playing St. Joan struggles to expose a murder. "...[Wilson's] best work since *Fifth of July*...An intriguing, prismatic and thoroughly engrossing depiction of contemporary small-town life with a murder mystery at its core...a splendid evening of theater..." *–Variety.* "...fascinating...a densely populated, unpredictable little world." *–St. Louis Post-Dispatch.* [6M, 5W] ISBN: 0-8222-1767-8

★ **THE SYRINGA TREE by Pamela Gien.** Winner of the 2001 Obie Award. A breathtakingly beautiful tale of growing up white in apartheid South Africa. "Instantly engaging, exotic, complex, deeply shocking...a thoroughly persuasive transport to a time and a place...stun[s] with the power of a gut punch..." *–NY Times.* "Astonishing...affecting ...[with] a dramatic and heartbreaking conclusion...A deceptive sweet simplicity haunts THE SYRINGA TREE..." *–A.P.* [1W (or flexible cast)] ISBN: 0-8222-1792-9

★ **COYOTE ON A FENCE by Bruce Graham.** An emotionally riveting look at capital punishment. "The language is as precise as it is profane, provoking both troubling thought and the occasional cheerful laugh...will change you a little before it lets go of you." *–Cincinnati CityBeat.* "...excellent theater in every way..." *–Philadelphia City Paper.* [3M, 1W] ISBN: 0-8222-1738-4

★ **THE PLAY ABOUT THE BABY by Edward Albee.** Concerns a young couple who have just had a baby and the strange turn of events that transpire when they are visited by an older man and woman. "An invaluable self-portrait of sorts from one of the few genuinely great living American dramatists...rockets into that special corner of theater heaven where words shoot off like fireworks into dazzling patterns and hues." *–NY Times.* "An exhilarating, wicked...emotional terrorism." *–NY Newsday.* [2M, 2W] ISBN: 0-8222-1814-3

★ **FORCE CONTINUUM by Kia Corthron.** Tensions among black and white police officers and the neighborhoods they serve form the backdrop of this discomfiting look at life in the inner city. "The creator of this intense...new play is a singular voice among American playwrights...exceptionally eloquent..." *–NY Times.* "...a rich subject and a wise attitude." *–NY Post.* [6M, 2W, 1 boy] ISBN: 0-8222-1817-8

DRAMATISTS PLAY SERVICE, INC.
440 Park Avenue South, New York, NY 10016 212-683-8960 Fax 212-213-1539
postmaster@dramatists.com www.dramatists.com